A MARKET THEORY OF MONEY

A MARKET THEORY OF MONEY

JOHN HICKS

CLARENDON PRESS . OXFORD

1989

Oxford University Press, Walton Street, Oxford OX2 6DP

Oxford New York Toronto
Delhi Bombay Calcutta Madras Karachi
Petaling Jaya Singapore Hong Kong Tokyo
Melbourne Auckland

and associated companies in
Berlin Ibadan

Oxford is a trade mark of Oxford University Press

Published in the United States
by Oxford University Press, New York

British Library Cataloguing in Publication Data
Hicks, John, 1904
A market theory of money.
1. money. Theories
I. Title
332.4'01
ISBN 0–19–828724–0

Library of Congress Cataloging in Publication Data
Hicks, John Richard, Sir, 1904–
A market theory of money / John Hicks.
1. Money.   I. Title.
332.4'01—dc20   HG221.H633 1989   89–3364
ISBN 0–19–828724–0

Filmset by Eta Services (Typesetters) Ltd, Beccles

Printed in Great Britain by
Bookcraft Ltd.
Midsomer Norton, Bath

CONTENTS

transferability. Shareholder and bondholder. Why buy shares? Why issue shares? Why pay dividends? Take-overs and mergers. Uses and misuses.

Part III

PROBLEMS AND POLICIES

This rather detailed table of contents has been devised to take the place of an index, which for a book of this character proves to be inappropriate.

Introduction

Once upon a time I was giving a lecture, based upon my *Theory of Economic History*. When it was over, I was asked: are you a follower of Marx, or of Adam Smith? I am glad that I replied, without hesitation: both! Certainly I had learned something from each of them. Here, if I were asked a similar question—are you, or are you not, a Keynesian?—I should want to give a similar answer. For although, as will be amply shown in the following pages, I owe a great deal to Keynes, I also owe much to some of his predecessors, whom he thought to have made back-numbers; and also to some later writers, who were none of his 'school'. My own writings on money do indeed go back to the days when his were innovations. I was one of those who had to be converted. Perhaps, I have now come to think, I allowed myself too much to be converted. I already had some of the means to preserve a greater degree of independence, as I think will here be shown.

What was the essence of the 'Keynesian revolution'? I would now state it in the following way. It had been a common assumption of his predecessors that the economy under study had a 'long-term equilibrium' about which it would indeed fluctuate, but the fluctuations would be limited and by wise policy their amplitude could be damped. I think I can show that this was in their day a defensible position; in the days of the old Gold Standard it made a good deal of sense.[1] By the time Keynes was writing his *General Theory* that standard was being abandoned; by his 'persuasions' he had contributed to its abandonment, especially to the abandonment of its old authority; he had no desire to go back to anything so rigid, so firm. Thus the only equilibrium which survives in his theory is a short-term equilibrium, with no sheet-anchor to hold it.

It was not easy for those who were in my position, in 1936–7, to accept this abandonment. So the version of Keynes which we received into our own thinking was provided with another anchor, a

---

[1] As I shall be explaining in Chapter 11. Thus I would not want to go so far in attacking it as Kaldor did in his last book *Economics without Equilibrium*, though there is much that he said with which I am in sympathy. He sent me a copy of that book, inscribed 'as a token of a life-long friendship'.

supposedly constant level of money wages *in conditions of less than full employment*. There were particular reasons why at that date such an assumption appeared to be tolerable (they are discussed in Chapter 4). If it was accepted, the presentation of Keynes's theory could be greatly simplified. There was one way of doing this which I myself put forward, and which has been widely accepted. It is what has come to be known as the ISLM diagram, which has found its way into so many textbooks.[2]

Later experience has made this assumption untenable. For when after experience of, or approach to, Keynesian full employment, wages had broken loose from these moorings, product prices would rise and wages would follow, not because of a scarcity of labour, but in an attempt to maintain *real* wages, as would then be thought to be 'fair'. Money wages and the consumer price-index would be chasing one another. An orthodox Keynesian would then be obliged to say that what the plain man would call a high level of employment would in his terms be over-full employment; it would have to come down to a lower level if the 'inflation' was to be stopped. There would be no monetary (or fiscal) measure by which this disagreeable conclusion could be avoided. So the issue appears to be one of real wages, which the pre-Keynesians had thought that they understood. So does one come back to what Keynes called 'classical' economics?

I do not however believe that even in terms of economic theory that is good enough. For the pre-Keynesians were themselves not good at the problem which is thus thrown back at them. This was chiefly because they had no proper theory of markets. (The Walras model, which has become so popular with modern and especially mathematical economists, requires a form of organization which has rarely if ever existed.) I have therefore decided to begin this book, which is mainly to be concerned with a refurbishing of monetary theory (largely Keynes's monetary theory), with four chapters on the Working of Markets, not particularly monetary, but designed to fill a gap which was left by his 'classics'. Money, I consider, is a device which facilitates the working of markets. So these chapters are presented here as a prologue—a necessary prologue—to the more strictly monetary chapters which follow them.

---

[2] It appeared, though with different lettering, in my paper 'Mr Keynes and the classics', originally given to a meeting of the Econometric Society in Oxford in September 1936 and published in the journal of the society in 1937.

There is nevertheless another difference between Keynesian and pre-Keynesian theories which is not attended to in these chapters. As a consequence of abandoning their long-term equilibrium he confined attention to the short-term consequences of changes, such as policy changes. His predecessors had not been very good at that. Still the Keynes theory suffers from its inability, or disinclination, to look further ahead. A main way in which this shows up is in its concentration of attention on the employment-creating power of investment expenditure, *while it is occurring*. This will be much the same whether the expenditure is productive or unproductive. His 'investment' is just the use of current resources for purposes *other* than furthering the present or near-future output of consumption goods (or services). It will be just the same if it takes the form of building power-houses or of building palaces for kings. Its effect on productivity in the longer run is left aside. That does need to be remembered, even if we abstain from thinking in terms of *long-run equilibrium* (I shall come again to this matter in Chapter 13).

I began to write this book in 1985, soon after the death of my wife, who had been my fellow-worker for fifty years. It has been written in monastic seclusion, without the benefit of continual discussion. It is true that I have sometimes been able to get to meetings, sometimes far away, when I could get friends to help me. There are a few particular points which I owe to people I have met at those meetings; they are acknowledged as they come up. There are just three general acknowledgements I want to make. The first is to Axel Leijonhufvud, who started me off on this undertaking, convincing me that what I said on earlier occasions was not enough. The others are to Anthony Courakis and to Stefano Zamagni, without whose support and encouragement I could not have finished the book. None of them has any responsibility for what has finally emerged.

I am well aware that there are many articles which have appeared in journals, during the years while I have been writing, and earlier, which are relevant to what I am saying; I regret that in my circumstances I have not had much access to them. So I must leave it to their authors to discuss the relations between us—the other way round.

So for whom am I writing this book? Not for economic advisers, and commentators on current affairs, who have had opportunity to learn from experience much of the substance of what I am saying.

More for teachers of economics; I hope I shall help them to match what they say on one day with what they say on another. And for their critically minded students, some of whom will be the teachers of the next generation.

PART I

THE WORKING OF MARKETS

1 Supply and Demand?

The theories about price-formation in competitive markets, that were available to economists at the time when Keynes was writing, had been the work of the so-called 'neo-classics' between 1870 and 1900. There were several of these and they did not fit together very well. All however accepted the distinction that had come down from Adam Smith, between market value and 'natural' or normal value, natural value depending on cost of production, market value on supply and demand. Market value would 'tend' towards natural value by adjustment of supply. It was accordingly held, for nearly a century after Smith, that natural values were the only values that required attention. The whole of Ricardo's system, to take the most important example, runs in terms of natural values.[1] The chief thing which happened at the 'marginal revolution' of Jevons and his contemporaries was a shift of attention to market values. They were determined, it was accepted, by supply and demand; but how? Just how did the market work?

Though Jevons (1871) saw the problem, he failed to solve it. He gave nothing better than a rather simple-minded mathematician's answer: that if the article being sold was of uniform quality, there could not be more than one price in the market, so the price must be that at which the last (or marginal) unit would sell (his 'law of indifference'). As is obvious to the modern student, this implied that the market was always in equilibrium. But how did it get into such an equilibrium? Jevons gave no help.

Walras (1874), writing without knowledge of Jevons, met the same problem; he also gave a mathematician's answer, but his was more subtle. The price must be established at the level where curves showing demand and supply, as functions of price, intersect. But

---

[1] It may be objected that in his rent theory, Ricardo had the price of 'corn' determined at the margin, and so was dependent on demand. Nevertheless it is a *normal* price which is taken to be so determined; otherwise how did he fail to mention the weather? Ricardo is showing that in the case of an agricultural product, not market value only but also normal value is dependent on demand. The most Ricardian among modern economists was his editor, Piero Sraffa. It is significant that Sraffa's own theory (*Production of Commodities by means of Commodities* 1960) runs entirely in terms of normal values.

how are these curves to be found before there is any trading? If the equilibrium has not been found before there is any trading, much or most of the trading must have been conducted at non-equilibrium prices, so the average price over the day may be far from the equilibrium price; even the final price, at the end of the day, may be out of equilibrium. Walras's answer to the puzzle was to suppose all parties trading to disclose their propensities before trading started. The 'market organizer' (as I prefer to call him, for a reason which I give below[2]), when he had this information reported to him, could calculate the equilibrium price, and at that price actual trading could proceed.

Though it must be accepted that it is possible for a market to be organized in this manner (by some preliminary agreement between the parties trading) this particular form of organization is not one which at all commonly occurs. Neither Edgeworth (1882) nor Marshall (1890) were satisfied with Walras's answer, of which they were aware. Each of them supposed that information was collected in the course of trading.

What takes the place of Walras's organizer, in the market as analysed by Edgeworth, is ability to recontract. All contracts for sale are provisional. That is enough (when there is no monopoly on either side of the market) to show that a uniform price must be established; for if there were no such uniformity, a buyer who had bought at a high price could repudiate his contract, finding a seller who had sold at a lower price, to whom he could offer more favourable terms. Further, if at the uniform price thus established there were buyers who had not exhausted their demands at that price, or at any price in its neighbourhood, they could find sellers who had sold at the established price but who could be tempted away by an offer a bit better. Thus the market would come to an equilibrium with demand and supply, at the end, equated.

This solution of Edgeworth's was a great step forward; but it was unfortunate that the illustration he gave, with which to explain it, was not well chosen. This ran in terms of a labour market; it must be

---

[2] It should be noticed that the Walras market is *not* an auction market, with which it has often been confounded. Most auction markets are for second-hand commodities, such as pieces of old furniture or houses, of which each unit is to some extent unique, so that Jevons's law of indifference does not apply. The auctions which are nearest to the Walras model are those sometimes used for new issues on the stock exchange. But even in this case the auctioneer is an agent for the seller; he is not the independent organizer postulated by Walras.

granted that in that application it does not make much sense. (I shall be coming to the labour market later.) There are other markets, which do exist, where it works much better. All that is needed to make it realistic is to introduce intermediary traders, neither final buyers nor sellers, who on occasion may either buy or sell. So they are readily able to reverse their contracts. *Arbitrage*, which is precisely the kind of transaction on which Edgeworth relies to establish his uniformity, is common enough in practice for a name to have been given to it.

Edgeworth knew very well that the 'equilibrium' which is established in his way at the 'end' of the market need not be the same as that which would have been established in Walras's manner. For willingness to trade at the 'end' could well be affected by gains and losses due to non-equilibrium trading on the way. This is the point that was taken up by Marshall. In substance he accepted Edgeworth's analysis;[3] there was just one point, to which he seems to have attached considerable importance, which he added to it. If it could be shown that the gains and losses which will have attended non-equilibrium trading 'on the way' are unlikely to have much effect on the willingness of buyers to purchase an additional unit, will not the market finish up at an equilibrium price in the sense of Walras, after all? If these gains and losses amount to no more than a small part of the buyers' total expenditure, the 'income effect' (as we should now say)[4] of allowing for them should not be considerable. So the market should finish up at something quite near to a Walras equilibrium.

Marshall was very attached to this proposition of his; but it is not as helpful as he supposed. When he tries to write it out in a realistic manner, as was his custom, this shows up. He interprets it as the behaviour of a 'corn market in a country town'.[5] Various realistic characteristics of such a market are allowed to slip in; most do not matter, but there is one that is of fundamental importance. He had admitted among the characters of his story the farmers who bring the corn to market and the consumers (or millers?) who take it off, also merchants who act as intermediaries; all that, as we have seen, is as it should be. But it also allows his merchants to carry over surplus

---

[3] *Principles*, mathematical appendix, note XII.
[4] In Marshall's terminology, the 'marginal utility of money' would be substantially unaffected.
[5] Part V, Chapter 2.

stocks at the end of the day; and if at the end, why not at the beginning? What then is the significance of the 'end of the day'? A market in which carry-over is permitted is a continuing market; it does not 'finish up'.

When in the 1920s at Cambridge a new generation of teachers were set to lecture on Marshall, putting into their own words what he had said, this was one of the things that troubled them. If Marshall's proposition was to be used in the way he had used it, there could be no carry-over; so it would be safer to make the article traded perishable—'fish' not 'corn'.[6] That is formally correct, but it greatly reduces the scope of the theory. The Marshall market becomes a very special type of market, a little better but not much better than the artificial market of Walras.

What was then to be done? The right thing, surely, would have been to go on to construct a formal theory of the market for a non-perishable product; that indeed would have turned a corner. One could still have followed Marshall and admitted intermediary traders; and also have followed him in supposing that these were the people who held the stocks. Since they would have been willing to come in either as buyers or as sellers, there would be an 'inside' market which would develop between them. It would be on this inside market that a market price, variable not just from day to day but from moment to moment, could make its appearance. It was surely the theory of such a market which was the next thing which should have been formally set out.

It did not happen, just like that, for two reasons, one general, one more special. I take the special reason first.

It was bound to be noticed, as soon as the first step was taken along the road to such a theory, that the market in question would be a speculative market; and speculative markets, highly organized speculative markets, for some particular commodities, did unquestionably exist. But they also seemed to be a very special kind of market. Should they not also be regarded, like the 'fish' market, as a peculiar case? That was indeed the way in which they came to be regarded by Keynes himself. He had himself done some thinking about the working of such markets, and in his *Treatise on Money* (1930) he gives a good though incomplete account of them;[7] but

---

[6] I am sure it was Dennis Robertson who told me about the 'fish market'. I think he must have invented it himself.

[7] *Treatise*, Chapter 29 (in Volume 2).

the thrust of his chapter is to explain why such markets are *not* important—because it is only in exceptional cases that costs of stock-holding are low enough for large stocks, of a particular commodity, to be carried. So, in his *General Theory* (1936) he leaves them out. A gap was thus left, between the 'fish' markets, where carrying costs were prohibitive, and the regular speculative markets, where they were so very reasonable; into that gap a great number of actual markets must fall. And Keynes, in neither of his books, gave much help in dealing with them.

Then there was also the more general obstacle. The theory that was needed could not be developed without a considerable change in point of view. The traditional view that market price is, at least in some way, determined by an equation of demand and supply had now to be given up. If demand and supply are interpreted, as had formerly seemed to be sufficient, as flow demands and supplies coming from outsiders, it is no longer true that there is any tendency, over any particular period, for them to be equalized; a difference between them, if it were not too large, could be matched by a change in stocks. It is of course true that if no distinction is made between demand from stockholders and demand from outside the market, demand and supply in that inclusive sense must always be equal. But that equation is vacuous. It cannot be used to determine price, in Walras's or Marshall's manner. For what matters to the stockholder is the stock that he is holding; the increment in that stock, during a period, is the difference between what is held at the end and what was held at the beginning, and the beginning stock is carried over from the past. So the demand–supply equation can only be used in a recursive manner, to determine a sequence;[8] it cannot be used directly to determine price, as Walras and Marshall had used it.

[8] It is a difference, or differential, equation.

2 The Function of Speculation

An outline of the theory, which in the light of these considerations should have been felt to be required, may be introduced by going back to the corn market of Marshall. This is a closed system, so far as the corn is concerned; there is no trade with other such markets; all transactions are between the parties listed, producers, consumers, and dealers. But then, as Marshall in his pursuit of realism should surely have noticed, ought we not to think of new supplies coming on to the market at harvest-time, while demand is relatively steady over the year? Someone then must be holding stocks, high just after harvest, gradually falling to a low point just before the next. It is reasonable to suppose that they will be held by the dealers.[1]

We shall further find it convenient, for no deeper reason than convenience of statement, to suppose that the market is only open for one 'day' in each 'week'. Our market is accordingly endowed with *two* significant periods, the *week* which elapses between successive market-days, and the *year* which elapses between two successive harvests. These are different, not just in duration, but also in their relation to the working of the model.[2]

Any dealer, on any market-day between the harvests, has a choice between selling (to consumers or to another dealer) and holding on. If he is to do a bit of both, as some dealers must be doing if the market is to continue, the advantage he expects (or plans) to get at the margin from the two courses must be the same. Granted that there are some extra costs involved from holding longer,[3] it can only be profitable to continue holding a part of the stock in his possession, if the price he expects to get from selling later is higher than that which rules at the moment. If this expectation is realized, and goes on being realized, the market price must go on rising during the year—from a low point just after the harvest to a high in the following summer, after which it falls, as a result of the following harvest.

---

[1] For that is the arrangement which (usually) will minimize transport costs.
[2] They have very little to do with the 'short' and 'long' periods of Marshall, which he introduced at a later point in his analysis to that we are here considering.
[3] Cost of sale to consumers may (realistically) be reckoned to be borne by the consumers.

It is already apparent, from consideration of what happens in this very simple example, that there are two quite different senses of the term 'equilibrium' which are coming up. One relates to the week, the other to the year. It is perfectly proper to say that the market is in equilibrium during a particular week if the price established at the end of the week (at the next market-day) is the same as what was expected for it at the week's beginning. (This is the *ex-ante/ex-post* equilibrium of the Swedish economists contemporary with Keynes.) It is quite different from the flow equilibrium of Marshall and his predecessors, which in our case can only refer to the *year*. As we shall see, there is room for both.

For the market to be in 'Swedish' equilibrium during a particular week, when that is taken by itself, is not a very stringent condition. The foresight which is required is not considerable. It should further be noticed that it need not be stated in so 'subjective' a manner. For it only requires that the actions taken at the beginning of the week (holding stock or disposing of it) should be such as would have been taken if the end-price had been correctly foreseen. That is a matter which in principle can be tested. It is true that to suppose it to hold for all weeks within the year is a more serious matter. It does however lead to testable results. In our case it leads to the course of prices that was described—low just after the harvest, rising to a high point just before the beginning of the next.

If flow equilibrium is interpreted, after the manner of Marshall and his contemporaries, to mean a condition in which price remains unchanged because flow demand and supply are in balance, it is impossible in our model for the market to be in equilibrium *within* the year. It could however be in a flow equilibrium from one year to the next, to mean that there was an annual cycle which repeated. The conditions for this to happen are obviously very stringent. The stock must be the same just before the first harvest and just before the second; and also the same just after the first harvest and just after the second; both of these conditions cannot be satisfied unless the two harvests are equal. And also what is taken off by consumers in the two years must be the same. If the flow demands of consumers have *any* elasticity (their demands for corn are not absolutely inelastic) the price over the year, its general level over the year, must be such as to keep demand and supply in balance, over the year as a whole. But it is only because of the (seasonal) fall in price when the new harvest comes in that there will, in this equilibrium state of our model, be no carry-over from year to year. Only so can we be satisfied with what is shown in the conventional supply–demand curve diagram. In all other cases there is more to be considered.

Before we can properly trace the course of the price from one year to another, there is a little more to be said about the movement within the year. If 'Swedish' equilibrium is maintained within the year, the price must be rising just fast enough to cover the marginal cost of holding stocks. This is in principle composed of two elements, one physical, the other financial. The physical cost is the cost of storage, the financial is the interest that is given up on the funds locked up in the holding of the stock. Now it may well be maintained that in the full equilibrium state of our model, marginal cost of storage should be very low, for it is confined to the cost of measures that are needed to prevent some physical deterioration. Storehouses indeed will have to be provided, and they will have what may here be regarded as a rental cost; but this will be nearly the same whether the storehouses are full or nearly empty. So it may be that the main cost of storage, during the week, is interest cost—interest which could be earned, during the week, on the funds that are locked up in the holding of the stock. If the rate of interest is low, this need not be considerable; so the annual price-cycle should be nearly flattened out. (This means, incidentally, that the fall in price, at the time of the harvest—during the period of the harvest—need not be great.)

But now suppose that our model, having been for some time in this 'annual' equilibrium, is confronted, in some particular year, with a harvest which is not so obligingly 'normal'. The cases of an exceptionally large and of an exceptionally small harvest are substantially different, for though supplies can be carried forward in time, they cannot be carried back.

Take first the case of a deficient harvest. If there had been no news of the deficient harvest before the end of the annual cycle of the previous year, the difference which would be made by experience of the new harvest being deficient would simply mean that the *level* of price, over the annual cycle of the post-harvest year, would have to be higher. There would be no more to be said than that. If however the news came in earlier, before stocks left over from the previous harvest had been exhausted, there would be an incentive to hold them back from the market; so the price would rise *earlier* than it would otherwise have done. One can see that rise being blamed on 'speculation'. It would however do no more than smooth out a rise which would have inevitably occurred.[4]

In the opposite case of a more than normal harvest, anticipation of its appearance could not make much difference. For even if a normal harvest had been expected, a fall in the market price at the time when that harvest came in would have been expected, so the stocks which were held near the end of the harvest year would have been small; there would not be much that could be released in anticipation of a further fall in price. The major difference from the equilibrium sequence would come *after* the harvest. The problem with which stock-holders would then be confronted would be a matter of the future disposal of their (now) exceptional stocks. How much should be disposed of within the coming year? How much should be carried over to a further future? That would have to be decided, directly or in-directly, in the light of the way in which the appearance of the big harvest was interpreted.

If the big harvest was taken to be exceptional, giving no indication that future harvests would be anything but normal, it would be profitable to carry over some part of the supply to future years. But if it were read as meaning that future harvests also would be expanded to the new level, or thereabouts, there would be nothing to be gained from carry-over, so the price would have to fall sufficiently to engender a flow demand equal to the increased supply—just as in the textbook version of the story where no attention is paid to holding of stocks. (There would still be an annual cycle about this new level of prices.) If some dealers read the situation one way and some another, there would still be some carry-over to the further future; that would moderate the fall in the level of price in the year after the big harvest came in. The possibility of holding stocks over the future would be acting as a buffer.

But then, as soon as we admit such differences of opinion, other possibilities open. The optimists, as we may call them, who take the low price to be temporary, will be more willing to hold stocks than the pessimists, who take it to be permanent or more permanent. So why should there not develop an 'inside' market between the two classes, pessimists selling to optimists, in which (by arbitrage) a regu-

---

[4] Historical cases of this phenomenon, complicated and of course alleviated by some possibility of drawing supplies from outside sources, have been studied by A. K. Sen in his *Poverty and Famines* (1981).

lar market is established? That is indeed what happens on the speculative markets, which (as we saw) Keynes put aside as a special case.

The reason why it is special is mainly because of a further complication. The optimist buyer may not have the facility to take physical charge of what he (temporarily) acquires; he may have no storehouse at his disposal. What he requires is to have *proprietorship* in the article traded, so that he can sell it when he chooses to do so; he does not desire to have the *custody*. But how is proprietorship to be transferred without change of custody? Only, as commercial men have long discovered, by expressing the proprietorship in a document, which confers a *right*.

What is required here is that the right should be easily transferable; so its terms must be precise. A right to take possession of a particular stock, the physical condition of which will have to be ascertained at the time when the right is exercised, is not precise enough. Nor is it enough to leave any obscurity about the date at which the right is to be exercised. The practical solution is for the right to be expressed in a 'futures' contract, which takes the form of a promise to deliver, at a specified date, a specified quantity of a standard grade of the article traded. Such a promise is admirably suited for trading between dealers; anyone who acquires it can readily pass it on, at any time before its expiry, at a market price. The holder of a physical holding can then 'hedge' his position by issuing (or selling) a corresponding 'future' at a current market price; he is then in a similar position to that he would have been in if he had sold his actual stock forward to the date of expiry of the 'future', with the only uncertainty left consisting in the difference between what his actual stock is worth at that date, and the value at that date of a stock of standard quality. It is easy to see that he will usually be able to protect himself if the 'futures' method is adopted more cheaply than if he had proceeded by a simple forward sale, just because the 'future' is easily transferable. But for such re-arrangement to be practicable, there must be agreement among traders on the definitions of standard qualities; so the futures market must be an organized market, in quite a different sense from the organized market of Walras.

No more need be said in this place on the working of futures markets. For futures are not themselves commodities; they are promises to deliver a certain quantity of a commodity (or rather the *current* money value of that quantity, as it will be at the specified date). They are the same kind of thing as an indexed bond. It is in that connection, when I come to financial markets, that I shall have a little more to say about them (see Chapter 10). They come in here simply as one device by which holding of stocks may be made easier, so that the smoothing of price-movements which has been shown to follow from carry-over is facilitated. It is however the physical carry-over which does the smoothing; that can occur, to a significant extent, even in the absence of futures markets.[5]

For this reason it must be insisted that whatever is the practical importance of organized commodity markets, at one time (or place) or another, they need to occupy a central place in a general theory of markets, because they are the most sensitive markets we know. They are the practical counterpart to the 'perfect competition' models of the textbooks; but they do more for the economist than those models can do, because they bring out so forcefully that most prices are determined, not by mechanical matching of flow propensities, but by the way they are interpreted, thus by the state of mind of those who trade. There is not, at least there need not be, anything 'irrational' about this. It is just that knowledge of what may happen in the future can never be complete. In my 'harvest' model I have simplified this ignorance, since the date at which relevant information would come in (the date of the next harvest) was supposed to be known. In a more general case that also (or what corresponds to it) would be uncertain. This makes the stabilization more difficult but does not I think affect the principle.

The chief things which our model has shown, in spite of this simplification, are (1) that the stabilizing effect of stockholding is better for dealing with unexpected surpluses than with unexpected shortages, and (2) that it is better for dealing with moderate surpluses than with those that are large. For while the marginal costs of carry-

---

[5] This is surely a point at which I should make an acknowledgement to Kaldor, whose truly classic paper 'Speculation and income stability' (*R. Econ. Studies* October 1939, reprinted and revised in the second volume of his *Essays* 1980) has been of the greatest help to me in this chapter. I look upon it as the culmination of the work that was done in this field, not only by Keynes but also by Hawtrey, in the twenties and thirties. It has not received the attention it deserves, largely I think, because he plunged his readers, without much preparation, into the complexities of futures markets, which taken like that are ferocious. I am trying here to be more gentle. I should like to report that in the last letter I had from Kaldor, only a few weeks before he died, he told me that he knew that Keynes did read that 'stabilization' paper of his and planned to give it serious attention. But we know that from 1939 to his death in 1946 Keynes had other things to occupy his mind.

ing normal surpluses, such as those of our seasonal cycle, may not be very considerable, for dealing with an exceptional surplus new facilities, such as storehouses, are likely to be necessary so that marginal costs will mount up. It is this last which has led, in our day, to the vogue of 'stabilization schemes' in which the cost of holding a buffer stock is met in some way out of public funds. The price is then set by what amounts to a producers' co-operative. Since it is operated in the interests of producers, there is always a temptation to set it too high, so that stocks go on increasing and their costs mounting up. There is then no way in which normal production can be resumed unless the surplus is destroyed, or removed in some way or other.

3 The Pricing of Manufactures

Three reasons why speculative markets in commodities are a special kind of market have emerged from our discussion. They require, if they are to flourish, (1) that the article traded should be fairly standardizable, so that supply from one 'outside' supplier should be a good substitute for that from at least some others; (2) that dealings should be on a sufficient scale for the costs of some organization to be easily covered; and (3) that arbitrage should be possible, so that most of the participants must be merchants who may either buy or sell. It is easy to see that these conditions are most likely to be satisfied in the case of raw materials; even the 'corn' of Marshall's market would be a raw material for millers. Thus the market, so far considered, can be no more than one link in a chain of transactions, extending from primary producer (farmer or miner) to ultimate consumer. At each link of the chain there is work for intermediaries. We may begin by thinking of them as acting independently, though we shall find that it is of the greatest importance that by 'vertical integration' they may be brought together. It is accordingly suggested that in the simplest model of a production system we should make places for two sorts of intermediaries—one between primary producers and manufacturers (this being the stage to which our previous discussion should now be taken to refer), the other between manufacturers and consumers, what are commonly called the distributive trades. Since it is the resemblances and differences between these two sorts of intermediaries to which I now desire to direct attention, I shall venture to call these distributive trades *secondary* merchants, contrasting them with the *primary* merchants, who deal in primary products.

Even among the *secondaries* there may well be disintegration, wholesalers and retailers at least being distinguished. Wholesalers sell to retailers and buy from manufacturers; retailers buy from wholesalers and sell to consumers; that is the normal course of their trade. Retailers rarely buy from other retailers; wholesalers however may buy from other wholesalers, just like the merchants on a *primary* market. Each of them, unless he is dealing in a perishable good, will need to hold stocks. A retailer who allowed his shop to be emptied would soon be out of business.

For the purpose of the retailer in holding a stock is different from that which operated on the *primary* market. It has nothing to do with speculation, with carrying forward, in the hope that at a later date the price will be higher. It has nothing to do with movement of prices. It would still exist in a world where prices never changed. By setting up his shop, the retailer has given notice that he is ready to be a seller of a particular class of goods. The penalty for being 'sold out' is not mainly the loss of profit on the goods that might have been sold; it is mainly a loss of reputation, or goodwill.

It is not only at the stage of retailing that this reputation motive may make its appearance. In the *primary* commodity market it is probably at its minimum; for the dealer on such a market need not run out of stock, since at a price he can always replace. It is by making losses on unprofitable transactions that he may come to grief. The same could be true of the *secondary* wholesaler stage, to which I shall be returning shortly.

But what of the manufacturer himself? There are two kinds of marketable stock that he may be holding. (Half-finished goods, goods in process, will usually not be marketable.) These are stocks of materials and stocks of finished products.

If he has easy access to a *primary* market on which the goods he uses as materials are traded, he will not need to hold much in the way of stocks of materials. (The chief reason for holding them will be to avoid the extra cost of frequent deliveries.) For what he buys from the market he will pay the market price. The price that is formed, in the manner we have examined, on that competitive market will be just transmitted to him.

On the holding of stocks at the stage of finished product there is more to be said. We can indeed conceive of an economy in which the same would be true in the case of finished product as in the case of materials. The product, as soon as it was completed, would be sold to secondary merchants (wholesalers) at a price which was mainly determined by trading among the wholesalers themselves. The manufacturer would have little means of exercising a direct influence upon it. This would be the practically realizable counterpart to the 'perfect competition' model of the textbooks.[1] It is however not

---

[1] At least in the sense that the manufacturers would be 'price-takers', not making prices by their own decisions. The textbook 'perfect competition' model is of course a static or 'equilibrium' model; it is not concerned with adjustment to a changing environment, the problem with which we are here concerned.

surprising, especially when it is spelt out in this manner, that it should appear to the modern student to be very strange.

I do not believe that it need always have appeared so strange. (That is why it was able to get into the textbooks!) There was a time, perhaps including a great part of the nineteenth century, when the principal end-products of manufacturing industry were rather simple: cotton and woollen textiles, sold by the yard, tools (knives and forks and hammers), even some sorts of basic foodstuffs (flour and sugar).[2] It is true that these could be regarded, in a way that was going to be important, as half-finished goods, left to be used or made up in the home. As long as these were the chief sorts of goods in question, it would be quite appropriate and convenient for stocks of them to be held by the wholesalers.

I have elsewhere[3] suggested that this was the system which may well have been in Marshall's mind when he came to his *short-period* theory of the 'industry', a part of his work which had particular influence on Keynes. The *short period*, it may be remembered, is defined as that which elapses before the fixed equipment of the manufacturer has had time to adjust. 'The producers have to adjust their supply to the demand as best they can with the appliances already at their disposal.'[4] Such adjustments as can be made under this restriction are taken to be rather rapid. Some time must nevertheless elapse between the date when a decision to change the rate of output is taken and that when the actual change results. But it does not greatly matter how the decision comes about. It could be that the decision is made by the manufacturer directly on his own initiative, reacting to a change in price on the wholesale market (and having to take the risk that when the output comes to be ready the price on the wholesale market may have changed); or it may be the wholesaler who gives the order, at the price which is currently ruling on the wholesale market, himself having to take the risk that by the time the goods are ready the price may be changed. Not much foresight is

---

[2] An octogenarian, like the present writer, can remember those days. I think of going with my mother to do her shopping (about 1910). There were none of the packaged goods which are the principal contents of the modern shop. There were bins and jars from which the goods were taken out in ladles. Then they were weighed out, and the quantity purchased was wrapped up in thick blue paper. I would like my reader to imagine that; it is a condition which can exist, for it has existed.

[3] *Capital and Growth*, p. 53.

[4] Marshall, *Principles*, p. 376.

required to adjust to this trouble so long as the time taken by production is short.

If conditions such as these are granted, there is nothing in Marshall's *short-period* theory which seems to be open to serious criticism. It needs not raise any puzzles about 'laws of returns'. There is no need to assume that there is a single optimum output for which the plant is designed; it is better, being more realistic, to think of it as having a *regular* range of outputs (from x_0 to x_1) which it is reasonably well fitted to produce. It would then be a reasonable simplification to suppose that over that range marginal cost is simply running cost per unit of output, not including any contribution towards covering the overhead cost of the plant itself, and this could be taken as constant so long as the prices of primary factors are given. Call this running cost c_0. If the price that was offered for the product was less than c_0, to operate the plant at any intensity would be unprofitable. (That is not to say that the plant must be idle; if the low price is expected to be no more than temporary, there may be a gain in some sort of reputation or other to offset the loss.) If the price that is offered is greater than c_0, it will always pay to go to the top of the regular range (to x_1), for that is where profit is maximized, or loss (after allowing for overhead) is minimized.[5] The overhead does not have to be considered when the question is just one of the scale of production from a given plant.

If the price that is offered is well above c_0, it may pay to expand output above x_1, for x_1 may be well below capacity output (x_2). From x_1 to x_2 marginal cost is likely to be rising, so there should be a rising supply curve of output from the individual plant.[6] But Marshall does not need this refinement to get a rising supply curve for his 'industry'. It would be enough that there should be different plants with different levels of basic running costs (c_0), more of them coming into

---

[5] The borderline case when price = c_0 does not need attention.

[6] There are several reasons for this, which should be distinguished. In the first place, it is useful to have some spare capacity in case of accidents (this is analogous to the need for reserves, on which much will be said when we come to the financial sector). Secondly, even if no question of replacement of plant is at issue, it will require maintenance to keep it in order. The cost of that maintenance could be reckoned into running cost; it is easy to admit that this would quite generally rise when maximum regular output was exceeded. (A distinction between maintenance expenditure saved by temporary closure and by permanent would have to be noticed.) Thirdly (the most difficult, in practice as well as theory), there is the effect of over-usage, in excess of 'regular' output, on expected life of equipment, the 'user cost' of Keynes. For the value to be set upon this depends on expectations, of a future that may be far away.

production when the price that is offered rises. (Just as happens in Ricardo's model of agricultural production, which Marshall is imitating.)

I have thought it right to give this amount of attention to the short-period theory of Marshall, not just out of respect to it as a historical monument, but because of the considerable impact that it had had on later work, not least on a puzzling chapter of the *General Theory* itself.[7] Surely however by the time of Keynes the structure of production and marketing which it had assumed had become quite out of date. The typical end-products of manufacturing industry no longer consisted of objectively standardizable goods, which could be traded on competitive wholesaler markets; they had become much more various, new products and new varieties being continually devised.

There were indeed a number of economists who were attempting to construct theories to deal with this diversity; some of them were working in Cambridge, close to Keynes himself. Joan Robinson, in particular, was a leading member of Keynes's own circle. Keynes however made no use of her *Economics of Imperfect Competition* (1933). I believe that for his own work he was quite right to pass it by. For her theory, like most of the others than becoming available, was a static theory. It was confined to a comparison of states, in each of which there was a diversification already established. It did not show how an imperfectly competitive system would work; but that was what Keynes required.

There was indeed one economist who had attached himself to this group, who had seen the problem and made an attempt to face it. This was Roy Harrod. In his article 'Doctrines of imperfect competition' (*Quarterly Journal of Economics*, 1934) he tried to deal with it on Marshallian lines, distinguishing positions of short-period and of long-period equilibrium; no doubt it appeared too late for Keynes to be able to take advantage of it. Harrod himself was later to become dissatisfied with it; it was nevertheless the best thing in the field which was available to those who took part in early discussions of the *General Theory*. But the direction in which it led did not prove in the end to be fruitful.

One can indeed now see that the stumbling block in the Harrod theory was already present in the Marshall theory on which it was based. How did Marshall himself suppose that his industry was to get into his long-period equilibrium? It would have to be supposed that his firms, or those controlling them, were endowed with remarkable foresight. They would have to see the equilibrium coming, and adjust to it in advance. For if they got it wrong, they would have the wrong equipment and would have to start all over again. That is one reason why the long-period equilibrium of an industry is a less useful concept than many neo-classics (and Harrod) imagined.[8] It is better to go back to the start and enquire how it could have been that the diversification came about.

There must have been a sequence of occasions on which decisions to introduce new products had been made. The maker of such a decision would have been an entrepreneur or innovator, a character who has not yet appeared in our story. For the manufacturer who simply responds to a signal given to him by the market, doing so almost automatically, is not called on to innovate. Our entrepreneur has to devise a new product, make arrangements for manufacturing it, and also make arrangements to get it sold.

For since the product is specialized, no other manufacturer producing anything exactly like it, any merchant to whom he sells it directly must be dependent on him for supply. The merchant must thus be acting, in this part of his business, as the manufacturer's agent. So we have here an important example of the *vertical integration* previously noticed; manufacturing and selling come in substance under the same control.

There were two functions which we were attributing to our secondary merchants and their market: stockholding and price-formation. As we saw, they are nearly allied; so it is here. The selling department is able to set a selling price and make it effective by holding stocks. That is to say, it can do its own buffering; and can do it relatively easily, since producing and stockholding have been brought so close together. So the price that is set can be chosen, as a matter of policy.

It is of the greatest importance that while the Marshallian manufacturer was selling in the first place to professionals, who would be able to assess just what it was they were buying, it is now the pro-

---

[8] It should perhaps be underlined that this is not only a problem of manufacturing industry. It is a problem of any form of production which uses fixed capital on a considerable scale.

ducer himself who has to take responsibility for the quality, and use-fulness, of what he is selling; for he is selling, at least at the end of the chain, to a consumer who is not an expert. That is why at this point there is a function for advertisement, which is basically a promise about the character of the thing being sold. It is a promise like that which is given by the retailer, when he opens his shop. In each case it is given by a professional to a non-expert, so it quite ordinarily needs to do more than just give information. The attention of the customer has to be attracted, by a smart shop-front in the one case, by pretty pictures and suchlike in the other. But he has then to be persuaded to buy on the strength of the information given to him, including a promise, explicit or implicit, that the information is correct.

The price is one aspect of the offer that is made; there are some characteristics of other aspects which are shared by it. The chief is that it must not be changed arbitrarily, at a moment's notice. Arbitrary changes 'unsettle' the consumer. He may be taking time to decide to buy; so if, when he finally decides, he finds the price has risen against him, his confidence is lost, and the seller's reputation is damaged. And it can happen that there is a similar obstacle to price-reductions; they cast suspicion on the quality of the product, they suggest that something is wrong. Thus the diversified market had a tendency to be what I have called[9] a *fixprice* market, meaning not that prices do not change, but that there is a force which makes for stabilization, operated not by independent speculators, but by the producer himself.

It is important (as Okun[10] has emphasized) that the stabilizing is more effective against price-reductions than against rises; the latter can be put through without loss of reputation, if an objective reason can be given for them. The most obvious is a rise in costs, which has affected not only this particular producer, but his (imperfect) com-petitors also. What he must not do (as he so often seems to do in the textbooks) is to admit that he is putting up his price because demand has increased: 'I am charging you more, because I can get more out of you.' The other side to this is the lack of necessary response to a fall in costs. It is tempting, then, to take a monopoly profit just by taking no action. The only safeguard against that which is offered by a diversified market is the appearance of new varieties which, if costs

[9] *Crisis in Keynesian Economics* (1974), pp. 22–40.
[10] A. Okun, *Prices and Quantities* (1981).

in general have fallen, can be offered at an appealing price. I suspect that this is the main way in which (in normal conditions[11]) prices can come down in such a market.[12]

[11] Exceptions are (1) when there has just been a very sharp rise in prices, which has not had time to get established, and (2) when there has been a great fall in the prices of raw materials, on 'flexprice' markets. In the slump of 1921 both of these conditions were present, in that of 1930 only the second, and the fall in consumer good prices was much less.

[12] This should be reckoned by the economist as a fall in prices; but his statistician partner, who makes his price-index numbers on the basis of a physically unchanged bundle of commodities, makes it hard for him to do so. There can be little doubt that real incomes, over the present century, have almost everywhere risen much more than appears from the statistics.

4 The Labour Market

There remains one extremely important non-financial market which has so far escaped our attention—the market for labour itself. How does that fit in? How does, or rather how can, a labour market work?

It might have been expected that the author of the *General Theory of Employment* would have given some help towards an answer, but he gives us very little. Nearly all he says is negative, just that on the labour market there is no equilibrium of demand and supply. But demands and supplies of labour are flows, work to be done over a period, and we have been seeing that there is no inevitability, in other markets, that flow demands and supplies should always be in balance. A difference could be made up by variation of stocks. Labour however is not a stock that can be carried forward. As a Victorian economist once said,[1] it is 'more perishable than cut flowers', more perishable, we might say, than 'fish'. So if there is to be an equilibrium, a continuing equilibrium, with unemployment, something must be implied on what is happening to the unemployed labour.

At the time when Keynes was writing, provision for 'unemployment benefit' was being extended in many countries; so it was natural for his early readers, and many later readers also, to take it for granted that the unemployed were being supported by some kind of public assistance. So long as that continues, the unemployed would not need to find a way of supporting themselves, so they need not compete with the labour which remained employed. In the model, accordingly, the level of wages could be taken arbitrarily, as Keynesians often appear to take it. This would correspond, in practice, to the wage being fixed by the power and policy of trade unions.

On a wider historical, or geographical, perspective that was surely a special case. Joan Robinson, a leading Keynesian, found that it was when she started to think about India. Her 'disguised unemployment' was a fitting of Indian experience into a conventional Keynesian mould.

I have found it more instructive to begin the other way round.[2] For

[1] W. T. Thornton, *On Labour* (1868).
[2] At greatest length in my *Theory of Economic History*, pp. 134–40.

surely there were wages before there were trade unions. Consider for instance the labour market in Britain in the days of Adam Smith. Even then wages were beginning to coagulate into some sort of a pattern. We shall understand the wage-system better if we begin by considering how it could have started in those days, and then go on to see how, in what circumstances, and to what extent a trade union system could have grown out of it. (That is similiar to the procedure we found it useful to adopt in the case of the market for consumer goods; I shall follow that procedure here.)

A standard model of this early stage of development would show no more than a part of the whole labour force, or potential labour force, being paid wages; the rest would have been supported otherwise. They could be regarded in Marx's manner as a 'reserve army', but they need not be idle. They might be working on family farms (which could have been paying rent to a landlord, but would not be paid wages by the landlord) or they might be doing domestic work in a family home. In either case it is by family connections that they are being supported.

One can see that a considerable movement, from family work to wage-labour, would frequently be matched by a movement from country to town. It is in that context that I find it convenient to begin to consider it.

It is a matter of major importance that there are two ways in which the movement could occur—according as the initiative is taken by a potential employer, or by the immigrant himself. These are fairly distinguishable in practice, since if the initiative is taken by the immigrant, he must himself bear the costs of movement, so he must almost inevitably come from fairly near at hand; while if the initiative is taken by the employer, labour can be brought from afar. (There are exceptions to this rule when the movement is subsidized.) It will however not pay for an employer to bring labour from a distance, or expensively, unless it is expected that the new arrivals will go on working, for the employer who has paid for bringing them, for some considerable time. So their employment must be, at least to some extent, lasting or (as I shall call it[3]) established employment.

As for the people who bring themselves, they will have no such assurance. Some of them, perhaps most of them, will just make a precarious living by picking up odd jobs. Though they are paid for doing

---

[3] All possible alternatives have associations which I do not, for the present, require.

those jobs, there is no market on which a regular rate of pay can be formed. For there are no intermediaries who can 'make' a market; neither 'buyer' nor 'seller' is professional. If we stretch the term 'market' to include it, this is the most *dis*organized market that can be conceived.

Nevertheless, even after beginning like this, our immigrant can sometimes make progress. If he has brought with him some particular skill, or can persuade people that he has some particular skill, he can let it be known that he claims to be competent to do that sort of work. He can then open what amounts to being a shop for his services, and much of what I have been saying about retail trade will apply.[4] The quality (or standard) of the service provided cannot easily be stipulated, so it becomes a matter of importance to the seller of such services to establish his reputation; the price-policy which he adopts is in part a means to that end. To quote a low price is a means of entering the market, but it is the 'low' end of the market which is most easily reached in that way. To work 'up' the market is a matter of gaining reputation.

Accordingly even here there is a wide range of possible outcomes, between failure and success. Those who fail are on the edge of starvation;[5] those who succeed may make fortunes. It is indeed from those who succeed that the entrepreneurs, who become the employers of established labour, may well be recruited.

So let us look again at the *established* sector, where there is a relation between employer and employed which promises some continuance. The employer expects the employee to stay with him, at least long enough to make a wage-bargain on that assumption, and the employee the same. It is here that there can most obviously be a market on which a wage is competitively determined.

If the market is to be a competitive market, each must be free to change his partner. The employee must be able to go away if he can find what he thinks to be a better offer, and the employer to dismiss him if he desires to do so. But by making their contract, the two have agreed to work together; if it is denounced by either party, each has suffered a defeat. The loss of the worker who is obliged to look for

---

[4] The shops of merchants and the workshops of artisans may be found side by side, as I have seen them myself, in Isfahan, in the days of the Shah.

[5] I think of the London poor of the nineteenth century, such as figure in the novels of Dickens. Why were things so different, for most of that time, in the United States? I shall come to that question later (p. 34).

another job is no doubt much more severe than the loss to the employer, if the latter is only obliged to seek for a replacement; but when the dismissal is incidental to a decision by the employer to reduce the scale of his operations, that is bad for him too. Thus in all cases of premature ending there is at least some loss for each, a loss which is better avoided. So it pays to take some trouble, and even to incur some expense, in order to avoid it. There is not much that the employee can do by himself to protect himself except to 'give of his best', and that can be no more than a partial protection. The employer, on the other hand, can see that he pays a wage which is at least as good as what is being paid by his competitors, so that an employee who has become established is unlikely to be tempted away. This is surely the principal way in which competition works, in the *established* sector—not by actual change of partners, but by potential change.

I think one can show that this is a matter of major importance, that it is indeed the essential way in which the labour market, when it is an established labour market, differs from the markets in goods, which we have been considering hitherto. Competition on markets for goods works for the most part, as we have seen, in terms of actual transactions; this is particularly so when there are intermediaries, whose actual dealings 'make' the market. So much is sold, and such a price is given for it. But potential competition does not work through actual transactions; it works through the influence of ideas about transactions which might be made, but are not. On these various parties may have different ideas. It is here, I believe, that the single employer, confronted by an unorganized labour force, has his chief 'bargaining advantage'. It is simply that he can afford to be better informed, better informed about the alternatives which for this sort of labour are open. He is, in terms of our previous discussion, more of a professional than his employee. But his bargaining advantage is diminished if the employee also can find means of getting professional advice.

So this is the first way the trade union comes in. At this stage the function of the trade union official (and, still more obviously, of the shop steward) is similar to that which used to be attributed to the broker on the London Stock Exchange. There is little place for jobbers on a labour market, any more than on a fish market; but the brokering function, the provision of professional advice to the non-professional party, is needed to make the competitive market work.

But a manual worker, by himself, can rarely afford to pay for professional services; thus the obvious solution, in the market for established labour, is for a number of workers to get together, jointly employing an agent—collective bargaining. It could be that this just made the competitive market work more smoothly.

But like other economic activities this function is subject, up to a point, to scale economies, so the trade union is made more effective by increasing its membership; that leads on to a second stage. For here as elsewhere increase in size affords opportunities for monopolistic behaviour; by using the strike weapon, or threatening to use it, a union may be able to extract gains from employers and through them from their customers. But to analyse their actions in these terms, though it is tempting for an economist to do so, since he has his monopoly theory at his disposal (an essentially static theory, it should be noticed) does not bring out aspects of the problem which experience has shown to be of importance. Trade union members cannot easily be mobilized to take action, which is costly to themselves when they are on strike, just to get a relatively small gain in the ensuing period. So they are characteristically better at defence than at attack.[6] This has consequences that can be traced.

First, it is easy to resist a formal reduction in (money) wages; that is the most obvious. So it is that in a well-unionized market, a straightforward reduction in wage-rates hardly ever occurs, except on a few extreme occasions, mostly when the reduction is understood to be temporary, and employment could hardly continue at all without it.[7] Other methods of reducing labour costs will normally be preferred.

Secondly, there are what are nowadays called relativities. It could be that in a perfectly working competitive labour market, when the wage of one sort of labour rose, the wages of similar sorts would be drawn up with it. But that implies that there is a fairly easy move-

[6] This was not enough allowed for, though it got some attention, in the thumbnail sketch of trade union history in Britain, up to the date of writing, which I gave in Chapter VIII of my *Theory of Wages* (1932). That is not bad as far as it goes, for it is based on empirical work I had been doing in the years preceding (since 1925). But the accounts I have given in later work, such as 'Wages and inflation' (1955, reprinted in the second volume of my *Collected Essays*), are more mature.

[7] The classical example of this, with an arrangement of this sort being formalized, is the selling-price sliding scales which were used for the regulation of wages in British coal-mining between 1870 and 1900. This was a very fluctuating industry with labour costs peculiarly heavy; it was for a while accepted that labour must take its share in adjusting to the fluctuations.

ment, or transformation, of the one kind of employment into the other. If the movement is difficult, it will not happen without union pressure. But it is understandable that people should think it ought to happen; if it does not, that is 'unfair'. This gets extended to cases when movement, within the period for which the wages are to run, is quite impossible; so it turns into a pressure for many wages to rise when some wages are rising.

These two taken together could be sufficient to account for the wage-inflation, or threatened wage-inflation, which has been with us, in so many countries, since 1945. Even if it is not resisted, it need not (so we are told) lead to price-inflation, if there is a sufficient rise in productivity. But it is quite independent of whether or not there is a rise in productivity, so it would not be surprising to find that it generally soaked through to price-inflation. But for that there has in fact been another source, the desire to defend not just a money wage, but a real wage, the money wage deflated by a price-index.

It is often said by economists that it is real wages in which trade unions should be interested, not money wages. But the fact is that until the beginning of the present century, there were no consumer price-index numbers, so there could be no question of an appeal to them; but quite strong trade unions go further back. All that could then be noticed by trade union members and their representatives were sometimes rises in particular prices, due to recognizable causes. It was not easy to base upon these claims for rises in wages in quite different industries.

The beginning of a change was in World War I. The general rise in prices, due in the first place to war-time shortages, was reflected in the (still very primitive) index numbers that were beginning to be available; it was clearly an element that had to have attention in wage-bargaining, sometimes going so far as to attach the money wage to a cost-of-living index. But that was taken at first to be just a matter of war-time disturbance. It must nevertheless have facilitated the great *fall* in money wages which occurred in Britain in 1921–2, when the wage-index (with 1914 as 100) fell from 280 in 1920 to 194 in 1923. Though that was matched with a corresponding fall in consumer prices, it was surely enough to disgust the trade unions with 'cost of living'. Little was heard of that in the later twenties and the thirties, when the price-index was steady or falling. So it was that when Keynes was writing, it was the maintenance of money wages for which unions were pressing, since that suited them better. It turned out to be most unfortunate that Keynes and his followers should have allowed this transitory state of affairs to be embedded so deeply into the structure of his theory.

During the Second World War, the experience of the First was repeated, but the sequel did not repeat, since (no doubt because of better management) there was no post-war slump. So there was no disenchantment with 'cost of living'. War changed to peace much more gradually, so war-time habits of thought did not so sharply disappear. It is conceivable that they could slowly have disappeared, so that the wage-system, like other parts of the economic system, could have been slowly steered into something more stable. In the British case, to which I cannot help referring (since it is that with which I am most familiar) it nearly was done. When I wrote about the matter in 1955, a good moment to be writing about it, I allowed myself to hope that this was going to happen, and for the fifteen years that followed it largely did. I quote what I said on that occasion:

The continual rise in money wages since 1945 . . . is sufficiently explicable in terms of factors that are peculiar to the time through which we have been passing. Especially during the last four years, the main factors pushing up wages have been (1) the dismantling of the controls, with its somewhat 'phoney' effect on the cost of living, and (2) the difficulty which has been experienced in the establishment of a new system of relative rates after the war-time disturbance. But these are difficulties which, in the absence of external shocks, we can expect to overcome . . . But it can hardly be doubted that any serious disturbance of our rate of progress would itself push the level of money wages in an upward direction.[8]

This is surely what actually happened in the British case. The 'good' years of the late fifties and the sixties were brought to an end by an external shock—a rise in the prices of several important imports, relatively to those of exports—which implied a reduction in the real wage that British labour was able to earn.[9] It was this which set off the following troubles. How much can be done in such an emergency, by monetary or semi-monetary measures, will be examined in later chapters.

But before concluding this, a little more should be said about the distinction, fundamental to my argument, between established and

---

[8] 'Economic foundations of wage policy' (*Economic Journal*, 1955), reprinted as 'Inflation and the wage structure' in my *Collected Essays*, Volume II (1983).

[9] It is very striking that in those good years the British terms of trade were nearly constant, while from 1970 to 1973 there was an adverse swing of about 20 per cent.

non-established, or less established, labour. I have tried to explain why trade unionism, and the 'social' influences on wages that go with it (for employers as well as employees are affected), are naturally characteristics of an established sector. The proportion of the labour force that is established can vary, from one time to another, and from one country to another. This is not just a matter of the degree of industrialization. It is by no means necessary that the whole of an industrialized labour force should be thoroughly established. It is possible to organize industry with no more than a nucleus of established labour, the rest of those who are employed in production being more loosely attached. Semi-skilled labour, which can be quickly trained to do its work, need not be tightly attached. Modern technology may well tend to make relatively increasing use of less attached labour. But I do not have the information to make more than a guess at that.

It is however worth noticing that if Britain (and possibly other European countries also) can be reckoned to have a long tradition of established labour, while in the United States the tradition goes the other way, much would fit into place. One can see, first of all, how it could have been that such a difference arose. In Europe, in the formative period, labour was being drawn out of agriculture into industry; and when people had moved, they could not easily go back. They had made a gain by moving, but a gain which they soon felt that they needed to defend. In the United States, on the other hand, the 'frontier' as it was called long remained open; there were also expanding opportunities in farming and in occupations ancillary to farming, so there was a two-way movement between the sectors. So the industrial worker had less need to defend his position; for if he were not paid what he thought to be a competitive wage, he would just go away. 'Exit'! Of course there were and are trade unions in America; but they have never sought to play such a part in the American economy as British unions have for so long in the British. That has repercussions which go very deep.[10]

[10] There are examples from other countries which seem to support this thesis, apparent exceptions which prove the rule. I think of Australia and Argentina, 'new' countries with very strong trade unions. Each has had a large, and for a while a growing, agricultural sector, but in each case the farming was highly capital intensive, which gave little opportunity for 'exit' from industry. The Australians have sought a release from their predicament by high protection; the Argentinians have failed to find even that. But I only mention these examples to show that they are not inconsistent with the general line of what I am saying.

It has for instance had its echo in the world of economists, making it hard for American economists and British (for example) to understand one another, not only on the particular matter of labour relations but more widely also. 'Search' theories of employment, which have had quite a success in America, do not in other countries have much appeal. 'Full employment', that sheet-anchor of the Keynesian system, looks quite a bit different according as one is thinking of the one sort of labour market or the other.

Keynes himself was surely thinking of employed labour as established labour; his unemployed were people who expected to be established but for the present were not. If their unemployment is only temporary, they will still have an eye on their established places; an increase in effective demand should bring them back, where they were. They would not have lost the capacity to fit into those places; they would have not just the skill, but also the use of the experience they had possessed. So if the Keynesian prescription was just directed towards helping a recovery from Depression (which is how many of its first readers including myself were inclined to take it) it is beyond question correct.[11] But it went on to claim that the same would hold if the Depression were long lasting; that, in the light of later experience, is less convincing. Perhaps it is more convincing in the case of the American-style economy, where most of those who are employed are less established; they will then have lost less in employability by being unemployed; if they are 'out', it is not hard for them to get 'in' again. The same may not be true of an economy with a large, very fully established sector, the sort of economy which we thought that Keynes had in mind.

I am getting short of words with which to explain myself, so had better have resort to adjectives which go better into symbols. Let us give the established employment the name *solid* employment or S-employment, and the labour which expects to get S-employment the name S-labour. Similarly, for the less established employment let us use the term *fluid* employment or F-employment, and for the labour which expects to get F-employment the term F-labour.[12] In our initial state of Depression, there is S-unemployment and F-unemployment. When effective demand is increased, according to Keynes, both S-unemployment and F-unemployment should be

[11] The only problem is financial—how to finance the expansion.
[12] We shall find it useful to use 'solid' and 'fluid' in ways that correspond, when we come to the financial sector.

absorbed. But suppose that for some reason (just a particular kind of technical change, or it may be that because of labour troubles employers would like to get out of employing S-labour) it is F-labour that is more readily adsorbed. 'Keynesian full employment' is then more quickly reached in the F-sector than in the other. Wages, as Keynes would expect, then start rising in the F-sector; and the rise carries over to the S-sector, on trade union principles, in spite of the unemployment which there persists. Further, since labour for F-employment does not need much training, it is drawn in from what was formerly outside the labour force (female labour and immigrant labour are obvious examples). So the labour force, as statisticians measure it, goes on expanding, and unemployment, as statisticians measure it, S-labour going on being substituted by F-labour, gets worse. The obstacle, it will be noted, is the blockage in movement of labour from S to F.[13]

Whether this is what has been happening, in Britain and perhaps in some other European countries, during the last ten years or so, is not a matter on which it is appropriate for me to pronounce. The business of theorizing, such as I am engaged in in the present work, is to ask questions and to formulate questions, not to answer them; still less to make recommendations on what should be done to meet the challenges which appear to have been raised.[14]

[13] A similar problem may indeed arise when there is increased demand for S-labour, but the demand is for S-labour to work in a different part of the country from that where S-labour is unemployed. Transfer of labour then implies transfer of residence, always expensive to the worker—made more expensive in current British conditions, by the subsidized or rent-restricted housing which is a hang-over from the welfare state of the years before 1980. A subsidy on stagnation!

[14] The Keynes theory on wages and employment, on which in parts of this chapter I have been commenting, has been taken in a form which is not exactly that in which it appears in his famous book. There he makes concessions to critics which, as subsequently appeared, he need not have made. This is most evident in his curious Chapter II, now known to have been written after the rest, in reply to criticisms which had been made on the other chapters by his Cambridge colleague Pigou. Pigou was arguing from a fully Marshallian position, on the formation of prices of manufactures, that in the 'short period' an increase in demand must raise their prices. So if money wages are given, an increase in 'effective demand' must lower real wages. Pigou maintained that it was this reduction in real wages which raised employment. Keynes, accepting that this would happen, claimed that Pigou had got the chain of cause and effect the wrong way round. All this would have been quite unnecessary if it had been accepted that (as I have tried to show in the preceding chapter) there is likely to be an important phase in recovery from depression, when firms who have been holding their selling prices to what they think to be a normal level, have no incentive to raise them when demand returns to normal. Over a range, that is, they will operate in a 'fixprice'

manner. This was brought home to economists, soon after the GT was published, by the work of J. T. Dunlop ('The movement of real and money wage rates', *Economic Journal*, 1938) and M. Kalecki (*Essays in the Theory of Economic Fluctuations*, 1939). I do not claim that when I published my version of Keynes in 1937 (what has since become known as the ISLM diagram) I had myself got clear on the matter. It was just that I saw that the best way of simplifying Keynes was to take money wages (provisionally) to be constant. I am grateful for the help I have had from Professor Tom Wilson on this matter.

PART II

MONEY AND FINANCE

5 The Nature of Money

It will no doubt have been taken for granted that in the markets we have been discussing, the typical transaction was an exchange of some article (good or service) for something that was recognized as being money; and it may also have been taken that the money was simply handed over, as one does when one buys a newspaper in a shop. A useful way of introducing the monetary theory, which will be the subject of the chapters which follow, is to begin by calling into question these two assumptions, asking how far they are justified.

Is is convenient to start with the second. It is clear from the most common personal experience that *spot* payment—payment 'on the nail' or 'on the spot'—is by no means the only, or perhaps even the most important, way of doing business. I may pay spot for a newspaper as I walk along the street, but I may also give an order to a newsagent to deliver a copy to my house each morning. I should not then pay for each issue as I received it; I should wait until the end of the month when he sent in his bill. At that time I should have been in debt to him for the papers I had got from him; the payment I made to him would have been in settlement of a debt. Surely it is the latter which should be taken as the general form of a transaction (of sale or purchase); it covers the case of the spot transaction, when the debt is settled immediately; but there arc many more complicated transactions it also covers.

It is probably true that it is only for small transactions—small, that is, from the point of view of one or other of the parties concerned—that the spot method of payment is ordinarily preferred. People are not, and never have been, in the habit of carrying about them a sufficient quantity of coin or notes to pay for a house or to pay for furnishing it. Even if the notes are of large denomination it is unsafe to carry them about without precaution. Further, when the article is of considerable value, the right of ownership in it has to be transferred; arrangements, usually legal arrangements, have to be made to get the transfer recognized. Each of these considerations tells against the use of the *spot* method. In transactions between firms which, as we have seen, are likely to be a considerable proportion of all transactions, each applies.

I shall therefore insist on regarding the representative transaction, of sale or purchase, as in principle divisible into three parts. The first is the contract between the parties, consisting of a promise to deliver and a promise to pay (both are needed to make even a constituent part of a transaction); the second and third consist of actual delivery, one way and the other. In the case of the spot transaction, all are simultaneous; but they do not need to be simultaneous. If there is any difference in timing, promises precede deliveries; that is the only rule which applies throughout. Delivery of the article may come before it is paid for, as in the case of 'consumer credit'; or it may come after, or partly after, as when the buyer 'puts down a deposit'. All of these are conveniently covered.

What remains, in general, immediately after the making of the contract, are on the one hand a debt 'in real terms' from the seller and on the other a debt in money terms from the buyer. Money is paid for discharge of a debt, when that debt has been expressed in terms of money. Thus money comes into the transaction in two ways, first in the part it plays in formation of the contract, then in the part it plays in paying. Do not these correspond to the classical functions of money, as laid down in textbooks, to be (1) a standard of value and (2) a means of payment? By taking the representative transactions in the form proposed, we have put them into their places in relation to one another.

What however of the third 'function', usually taken to go with them, of being a *store of value*? That money, on occasion, can be a store of value—that, as one used to say, it can be hoarded—is of course not to be denied. But this is no distinguishing property of money as such. Any durable and resellable good can be a store of value. A picture by an Old Master can be a store of value, but no one would want to say that it was money. Nor can money be distinguished, along this line of thought, by saying, as Keynes did, that money is the perfect store of value, that it is the only asset which possesses perfect liquidity, so that it does not have to bear interest in order that it should be held. For liquidity in turn cannot be defined, as we shall have much reason to see, except in terms of exchangeability for money. So to define money as an asset with perfect liquidity is to argue in a circle. It is the other functions of money which are intrinsic; the liquidity property follows from them.

A fourth 'function', to be a 'standard for deferred payments', has by the arrangement here adopted already been covered. It is included in 'standard of value' if, as I am supposing, payment is usually more or less deferred. 'Unit of account', which has often been taken to be a synonym for 'standard', accordingly says much less than what is needed.

We seem thus to be left with two distinguishing functions of money: standard of value and medium of payment. Are they independent, or does one imply the other? It is not easy to see that there can be payment, of a debt expressed in money, unless money as standard has already been implied in the debt that is to be paid. So money as means of payment implies money as standard. But could a debt expressed in money be discharged otherwise than in money? Surely it could.

It could for instance be set off against another debt, the debt from A to B being cancelled against a debt from B to A. If the two debts have arisen from similar transactions, the net result is a barter transaction, an exchange of goods with no money changing hands. That can happen, even if the debts are expressed in money terms; it is what has in effect happened, in international trade, on many occasions in the present century, particularly in Eastern Europe. There have been two countries which have run out of supplies of an internationally acceptable money, but have kept trade going between them by a more or less successful offsetting of debts. The debts are expressed in a money which is recognized by each of them but maybe not by others. Though this is called a barter deal, it is different from the small-scale swaps that figure in economic textbooks (such as the 'nuts for apples' in Marshall's barter appendix); for these make no use of money, even for acounting purposes. In the international barter deals, money remains as a standard, at least as a unit of account. It is money as a means of payment that is missing.

I will match that fairly recent example with another, also I think illuminating, from much further away. There have been societies, so anthropologsts in particular tell us, in which cattle have been used as money. What is the evidence for this? It is not like the evidence for coins, where actual coins have come down to us; it is not derived from bones of cattle that have been dug up. It is derived from what are in essence legal prescriptions, expressed either in written documents or in oral tradition, which set out the fines or compensations which are to be paid on particular occasions, as for offences of various types. If these are expressed in terms of cattle, it need not be supposed that they had always to be paid in cattle. The prescriptions are price-lists; they depend upon a notion of what things are worth. The things which were delivered in payment had to have recognized, or at least acceptable, values. (And values, it should be noticed, which were fairly unchanging over time.[1])

Indeed, as both of these examples show, the function of money as a standard, if it is no more than a standard, is to make it possible to form a price-list, in which the values of a number of commodities are reduced to a common measure. Without its help, there would be a distinct price-ratio between each pair of commodities, and these would not need to be consistent with one another. And that is a need which (as the cattle example shows) can arise without arising from trading; and (as the other example shows) can also arise from trading between two parties, none others being, even indirectly, concerned. It does indeed seem proper to lay down that barter, in the narrow or even in the wider sense, is appropriate only for bilateral trading.

Bilateral trading, as every economist knows, is an inefficient way of trading; it is at the gateway to multilateral trading that we come to money as means of payment. One might indeed conceivably construct a model in which the effect of multilateral trading was achieved through a sequence, or circle, of bilateral barter transactions. But it would be a very artificial model and we may be sure that if anything like it was ever achieved in practice, it would soon break up. For, as we have seen in Chapter 2, a competitive multilateral system depends on the activity of intermediaries, or merchants who are ready either to buy or to sell. Here, as in other activities, there are gains to be got from specialization; so we may think of the individual merchant coming to trade in a particular line of goods. These are the things he buys and sells; but for what is he to sell them? From whom and to whom is he to buy and then sell? It cannot always be merchants who have exactly the same specialism as he has, for that would get him nowhere. It must in the first place be merchants who have other specialisms, though the whole body of merchants will have dealings 'outside'. At least for dealings between merchants, a medium of payment is needed which is not a speciality, something which is acceptable by a merchant just because he is a merchant, so

---

[1] So the practice seems to depend upon some notion of a *justum pretium*, a proper or normal price. This is a notion which indeed is comfortable, still remains comfortable, in a legal environment. It is congenial to a lawyer to take prices from precedent, since that is what he does with other things. It is hard for him to accept the fluid prices which are formed on markets.

it must be something which can be readily passed on to a trader of any sort. That the precious metals, gold and silver, should have been found to be the most suitable commodities for this purpose depends on physical characteristics which are set out in all the old gold stand-ard textbooks; they need not be repeated here. What is important is that they were surely able to establish themselves through 'market forces'; no one had to order that they should be used in that way.

There was nevertheless a most important step, on the way to the establishment of a metallic medium of payment, which had still to be taken: the invention of coinage, which appears to be traceable to lands of Greek culture, about 650 BC. A coin is a piece of metal that has been stamped by the issuer; by the stamp it is guaranteed. The guarantee was in the first place one of weight and fineness, of quant-ity and of quality. In its absence the metal would have to be tested, in ways that were bound to be expensive, almost every time that it was used as money. That would have greatly impeded the use that could be made of it. (We do however have evidence that, at least some-times, transactions were conducted in this way; for hoards of pieces of uncoined silver have been discovered—archaeologists call them 'dumps'.) Coinage was a great step forward from that.

The stamp, in practice, has nearly always taken the form of an image, or emblem, of some ruler; the guarantee that is given is a state guarantee. How did that come about? Did it have to be a state guar-antee? It had to be given by someone, and there would seem to have been only three alternatives: it might be given by one of the mer-chants, it might be given by some sort of association set up by mer-chants, or it might be given by the government in whose territory the merchants were working. One can see that the second of these, if it were available, would be better than the first, since the circle of people who might be expected to have faith in the guarantee would be wider; and the third, again if it were available, should for the same reason be better than the second. So it is not surprising to find that it was the third which won out.

But the fact that a guarantee was given did not mean that it was always to be relied on; one does not get the impression that the kings of olden times were a reliable lot. So it was that in practice metallic money had many adventures. They make quite a story; it is eco-nomically interesting, but I shall not pursue it here.[2] It is sufficient to

[2] I have said most of what I have to say about it in my *Theory of Economic History* (1969), pp. 64–8. The chief thing which emerged from that discussion is that there

emphasize that metallic money, if it was to be usable, depended on a guarantee. In that respect it does not differ so much from paper money as is often supposed.

I shall instead follow up another development, already implied in the foregoing, from which, as we shall see, modern moneys were indeed to be evolved.

can be no assurance that a guarantee will be kept if the guarantor has a monopoly position; the effort, often made by rulers, to prevent the export of the precious metals was an effort to protect their monopoly. So it was that governments tended to be better behaved in this monetary matter when external relations were of major importance to them, or to the peoples over whom they ruled. This holds for the mercantile republics of Venice and Holland, and came to hold for England also. What appears to be a striking exception to this rule, the centuries-long stability of the gold coinage of the Byzantine Empire, may be less of an exception than it looks; for it would be explained by the dependence of those emperors on mercenary soldiers, coming from abroad and returning. (It appears that many of the Saxon army, defeated by William at Hastings, took service at Constantinople.)

6 The Market Makes its Money

We have seen that one way in which a debt can be discharged is to set it off against another debt. Debt is then 'paid' with debt. If there is a perfect match—the two debts, expressed in a common standard, being exactly equal—the net effect, as we saw, is a 'barter deal'. But there could fail to be a perfect match, yet payment by exchange of debts could still be feasible, if another debt could be brought in.

This would have to be a debt from some third party (C) other than the A and the B initially concerned. A is then asked to accept part-payment in the form of a debt from C to B, which is to offset the balance of debt between A and B, a balance we take to be in favour of A. But A can hardly be expected to consent to such an arrangement unless he considers that C is to be trusted. So there is a question of trust, or confidence, as soon as a third party is brought in.

But may not such a question arise even in bilateral trading? A is selling to B; each has promised to deliver; a time comes when A has delivered but B has not yet paid. It is understood that B has some time allowed him before he is obliged by the contract to pay; but it may happen that this time has elapsed and still he has not done so. How is he to be made to pay? The legal answer is that A then has the right to take back what he has delivered. But that (though, as we shall see, it has a part to play in the story) can easily fail to be an effective sanction; B may have hidden the stuff away, or may have consumed it. Nevertheless, if the transaction is not an isolated trans-action, but is part of a continuing business, there is another and often a better remedy: if one party to the trading defaults, the trade is unlikely to continue. That may be enough if the trading is bilateral; but if a third party, not concerned in that trade, is introduced, it cannot work. So the issue of confidence is chiefly one of multilateral trading.

In the standard economist's model of multilateral trading (the n-good m-person market of Walras) it is avoided; for there all transactions are spot transactions, taking place—somehow!—simultaneously. But if payments are made by offsetting of debts, and the debts are owing from different people, it cannot be taken for granted that all will be paid, or will be paid exactly when promised;

so the debts may well be of different *quality*. That need not prevent the establishment of a market in debts, a debt of low quality becoming exchangeable for one of higher quality at a discount. It follows that a trader, whose promises are judged by the market to be of poor quality, cannot get as much for his promises as he could if his promises were better regarded. So he has an incentive to improve the quality of his promises.

The quality of a debt from a particular trader depends on his reputation; it will regularly be assessed more highly by those who are in the habit of dealing with him, and know that he is accustomed to keep his promises, than by those who do not have the advantage of this information. Thus we may think of each trader as having a *circle* of traders around him, who have a high degree of confidence in him, so that they are ready to accept his promises at full face value or near it; there is no obstacle to offsetting of debts within that circle from lack of confidence in promises being performed. If he wants to make purchases outside his circle he will not be so well placed. Circles however may overlap; though C is outside A's circle, he may be within the circle of D, who himself is inside the circle of A. Then though A would not accept a debt from C if offered directly, he may be brought to accept it if it is guaranteed by D, whom he knows. D is then performing a service to A, for which he may be expected to charge. A would have to pay more for a guarantee from a trader who is 'further' from him; but he should often be able to get it at a reasonable price from some who are 'near'.[1]

We can recognize the market on which such prices are established as a market for *acceptances* of *bills of exchange*. I am taking that as the first of financial markets to be considered, not only for the historical reason that it is the first which we know to have flourished, but also because one can explain why it had to come first. Unlike the more familiar financial markets which will be shown to follow after it, it needs no specialists in financial dealings (bankers or even brokers) for it to work. It can come into existence through dealings between merchants (who may indeed be specialized in dealings on a particular line of goods, but are not specialized financiers); it can come about, without any particular attention being paid to it, in the ordinary course of trade.

Let us accordingly take that as the beginning and see what follows

---

[1] The mathematical reader, if there are such, may enjoy the parallel with his concept of analytical continuation in his theory of functions of a complex variable!

from it. We should be thinking of a fully monetized economy, which includes a sector of merchants, who use bills as media of payment between each other, while the rest of the economy uses cash, presumably coins. Then let the mercantile sector get large enough to develop opportunities for division of labour, on the famous principle of Adam Smith. There are at least two sorts of financial operators who should then begin to appear. One works within the mercantile sector, the other on the frontier between it and the rest.

The first are just intermediaries, with the regular function of intermediaries, in the market for bills. We should think of the mercantile sector as being made up of many, only partially overlapping circles, so that, in order to get the best value for a particular bill, a fairly roundabout route has often to be found. It is the business of this first kind of intermediary to find that route, getting a sequence of guarantees, as cheaply as possible.

The other kind of intermediation, which has more of a future before it, is the discounting of bills for cash. Any bill has a date of maturity, so it can (if it is honoured) be turned into cash simply by waiting. But the dates at which a trader finds himself in need of cash, to make purchases outside the mercantile sector, are unlikely to have a perfect match with the bills he happens to hold. So there is a need for intermediaries, between the bill market and the rest of the economy. They can only operate if they hold stocks, both of bills and of cash. Some at least must be doing so, so that when any one of them runs out of cash, he can replenish his stock of cash by selling to others.

For this to be easily and quickly possible, the quality of the bills he holds must be high; there must be no question of lack of confidence in them, no fear of default. So the effect of this second kind of intermediation is for the bill market to develop a 'core', consisting of 'prime' bills, as it should be appropriate to call them—bills which are such that there is no question of lack of reliability. That is a point at which most important things happen.

Until that point, the principal reason why the market value of one bill should differ from another is difference in reliability; but bills, between which no difference in reliability is perceived, may still differ in maturity. A trader who is in need of cash needs it now, not (say) six months hence. So there is a discount on a prime bill which is a pure matter of time-preference—a pure rate of interest.

I have chosen what may be thought to be this unnecessarily complicated way of introducing interest, because there is a reason why a simpler approach would not do. It is tempting to say that financial transactions are always, in some sense or other, loans; so the simplest form of loan contract—money being paid over now, in return for a promise of repayment, with interest, at some future date or dates—is the element from which we should start. One could start that way, and go on to admit that the amounts, and dates, of repayment may be not fixed but conditional on things that may happen in the future; so proceeding to insurance contracts, subscription to equities, and so on. Much of the matter we shall be proceeding to discuss could be reached if one started that way.

The trouble is that the establishment of a competitive market for simple lending is not at all a simple matter. The lender is paying *spot*, for a promise the execution of which is, by definition, in the future. Some degree of confidence in the borrower's creditworthiness—not just his intention to pay, but his ability to pay, as it will be in the future—is thus essential to it. There cannot be a competitive market for loans without some of this assurance.[2]

We may suppose, in accordance with what was said at the beginning of this chapter, that any particular potential lender will have a circle of potential borrowers around him, whom he knows, and feels that he can trust. We can conceive that there will be competition between these borrowers for loans from him. And we can imagine that a particular borrower might be so fortunate as to belong to the circles of several lenders, so that he can choose between them. But for both of these conditions to be satisfied, without some further complication of the story, looks most unlikely. I accordingly maintain that a necessary, or nearly necessary, condition for the existence of a competitive market for loans is that there should be intermediaries, such as, in our discussion of competitive markets for commodities, we found ourselves obliged to introduce.[3]

---

[2] The rural money-lenders, who so obviously do not have confidence in the creditworthiness of those to whom they lend, who therefore charge usurious rates of interest, in order to have a prospect of profit in spite of their expectation that many of those to whom they lend will default, are of course a well-known phenomenon. But they do not form a competitive market. Their clients accept their terms because they have no choice.

[3] It may be that some of my readers, having personal experience of the way in which, at the present day, a bank will offer loans, to such people as students, with hardly any security, will doubt whether my emphasis on trust is not overdone. Why does the bank not charge such people a much higher rate than that at which it usually

Let us accordingly go back to our bills. The simplest model, on that approach, is the model we were on the point of constructing—an economy consisting of (1) a mercantile or commercial sector, which uses bills as means of payment among its members, and (2) an outside sector, which uses cash. Let us further, to sharpen the issue, admit that the bill-using sector has a complete system of guaranteeing bills, along the lines described, so that all the bills it uses are fully reliable. There will still, as we saw, be a need for a special class of dealer who will discount bills for cash. But has not the model then settled into a familiar form, these dealers being similar to dealers in foreign exchange? 'Inside' and 'outside' are like two countries, each having its own money. The determination of the rate of interest, or discount, on the bills is equivalent to the determination of a rate of exchange.

We have learned from experience, though it has not been easy to learn it, that the rate of exchange between two currencies, though it is affected by the *current* balance of payments between the countries which use them, is also affected by speculative 'capital movements', which are sensitive to expectations of the future course of the exchange rate. So it should be here. Consider the position of the exchange dealers, on the boundary between the sectors, who make it their business to trade bills for cash. Changes in their holdings of bills (taking the whole subsector of the exchange dealers together) come about in two ways: first on the initiative of traders who are not exchange dealers, whose *net* demand for cash will rise or fall according to the balance of their trade with the other sector; and secondly on the initiative of exchange dealers themselves, because of changes in their relative willingness to hold bills or cash. We shall find that this distinction runs right through the theory of interest. 'Classical' theorists looked only at the one, Keynesians only at the other. For a proper theory of interest, neither should be forgotten. I shall have much more to say about this in Chapter 9.

It may however already at this stage be objected: is there not a fundamental difference between the market for foreign exchange and our market for bills? The former, if it is a freely competitive market, may surely establish the rate of exchange at any level, high or low; but if our bill market is to be used as an approach to the study of

lends, on the usurer's principle? Surely because it hopes to persuade the young person to become a regular client. The transaction is similar to the offer of a free sample by a manufacturer. The price of zero at which that is offered is not in itself a market price.

actual bill markets, or 'money markets', it needs to incorporate a
reason why bills, in practice, nearly always stand at a discount in
terms of cash, the rate of interest on them being positive. A sufficient
reason, within our model, might perhaps be found in the consideration that bills are only acceptable *within* the mercantile sector, while
cash is acceptable within that sector and also outside. So whether the
mercantile sector is large or small, cash must always have a wider
acceptability.[4] But it is probably more fundamental that cash is a
standard of value ~~ ~~~~ ~~ ~ m~ans of payment, so it is fully money;
it is the standard in terms of which contracts are expressed and
enforced at law; bills, being only a means of payment, are no more
than quasi-money. The discount is the expression, l_ the market, of
this inferiority.

The purchaser of a bill is, in effect, making a loan to the issuer; he
is willing to lend, in this form, because he is assured, and those who
have guaranteed the bill are also assured, that the loan, when the
time comes, will be repaid. Bills have usually run for quite short
periods, at the most for a year or so; it is easy to see that such a
method of finance is peculiarly suitable for commercial enterprises,
the capital employed in which is turned over quite fast. The lender
has just to wait until the 'ship comes home'.[5] Even before that
happens, the bill is represented by the cargo, or some part of it, so
that the lender can think of himself as entitled to something more
than a promise; indeed, as we saw, he has something against which
he can exercise a legal claim. But it is surely the fact that the bill is
guaranteed by people who are known to the lender, people who are
within his 'circle', that gives him better security.

One can see that there would be people, not within that mercantile
sector, who would want to borrow (and possibly, though perhaps
not so obviously) to lend. Some of those wanting to borrow would be
private people, often no doubt quite wasteful borrowers, just wanting
to 'anticipate' an expected inheritance;[6] more importantly there

---

[4] I think this is not upset by the point, which is often noted by historians, that it
may be safer to hold bills, in transit from buyer to seller, since cash is more easily
stolen. (A thief, or highwayman, will not find it easy to cash a bill that has come into
his possession.) That is indeed a consideration which must have facilitated the growth
of a bill market; but one must conclude from what happened that it did not outweigh
the others.

[5] Problems of insurance, as the history also shows, are almost from the first involved.

[6] 'The long-expected death of some old lady . . . Who has kept us youth waiting too
long already' (Byron).

would be a demand for loans by the government itself. This would be typically a demand to meet emergencies (wars and other disturbances), expenditure on which it is nearly always hoped at the start will not be long continued; so the ruler needs funds to tide him over, in just the same way as a merchant needs them. So he would like to turn to the bill, or 'money' market. Kings, as a matter of history, have often attempted to get loans on these terms; but there have been two obstacles in their way, each arising from difficulty in providing a credible assurance of repayment.

One was that while the creditor of a private debt could take legal action to recover from a defaulter (and this, though as we have seen it was not very effective, was nevertheless some protection), it was harder to use the king's courts of law to recover from the king himself. This, though intended to be a protection to the king, actually made it harder for him to borrow. The other was that to cover expenditure by raising a loan, to be paid back later, was bound to set the prospective lender to worry: if he cannot get the money now, otherwise than by borrowing, why should he be able to get it when the time comes to repay? It was by finding ways round these obstacles that obligations of the state became 'gilt-edged'.

It so happened, in English history, that ways around them were discovered, more or less simultaneously. The Bank of England and National Debt were founded, together, in 1693–4. A National Bank was the answer to one of the difficulties; to borrow *long* was the answer to the other. But as the experience of other countries shows, the two do not need to go together.[7] Each requires particular conditions for it to work, but the requirements are different.

A National Bank, which need not be a Central Bank (the Bank of England can hardly be reckoned to have been a Central Bank for the first century of its existence) is an intermediary between the government and potential lenders, themselves most conveniently being the rest of a banking system. Since it is legally separate from the government (though it may be owned by the government) its debts are commercial debts, which in principle are subject to legal action. The government however in a sense stands behind them; so what this in effect amounts to is a way by which the legal privilege of the govern-

---

[7] The story in the United States (essentially no doubt because it was the States, rather than the Federal Government, who at first were the needy borrowers) has been notoriously very different.

ment as a debtor is indirectly waived. There is much that follows from that which I shall be discussing in Chapter 9.

In the absence of such an arrangement, short-term borrowing by government must be difficult, for the other reason; it will be taken for granted by a lender that when the time for repayment comes, the government will have no way out but to reborrow, so the trouble will start all over again. That can be avoided if it is faced from the start, if the lender engages himself to relend, that is to say, if he agrees to lend *long*. The promise is then more credible, since it should be easier for the borrower to repay in the form of a moderate, though continuing, interest payment, than to repay the capital sum all at once. That there have long been people who are willing to lend on those terms seems to be shown by experience; but it does not seem to be inevitable that there should be plenty of them. That can hardly be taken for granted.

How far it is the banking system which has come to the rescue is one of the things which will be considered in the following chapter.

7 Banks and Bank Money

What is a bank? This is a question which has lately become quite topical; is one sort of business or another to have the right to call itself a bank? But this is because of the rights and duties which have been conferred on banks by legislation; for the purpose of an enquiry such as the present, these may at first be disregarded. For surely banks existed before there were any such regulations.

So we must define a bank as a firm which does banking business. But what is that? There is one kind of near-banking business with which we are here already familiar—that of the exchange dealers on the edge of the bill market who discount bills for cash. As we saw, this amounts to making loans to the issuers of those bills. We have been thinking of the promise expressed in the bill being credible, mainly because it has been guaranteed by a number of merchants, but also because it has arisen out of a sale of goods, which in principle can be reclaimed if the buyer does not pay. We have seen that borrowing would be more difficult if the borrower could not give something of that assurance.

What then is to happen if trade expands, so that more bills are drawn, and more come in to be discounted? Where is the extra cash that is needed to come from? Any one of the dealers could get more cash by getting other dealers to discount bills that he holds. But the whole body of dealers could not get more in that way. They must get cash from outside the market; they must themselves become borrowers. But what is the assurance which they can give, if they confine themselves to the business so far described, to the outsiders who are to lend to them?

The solution was to combine this business with another sort of business, which in the days of metallic money we know to have already made its appearance.

In excluding 'store of value' from definition of money, I did not of course mean to deny that money, any sort of money, could be hoarded. It would be quite rational to hoard it as a reserve against emergencies—the 'precautionary motive' of Keynes. But hoarding of gold or silver would not have been a simple matter. There would always have been a problem of keeping it safe from theft or pillage, and yet accessible to the owner, so that he could lay hand on it whenever he wanted it. The obvious solution was to entrust it to a custodian, who could make expert arrangements for looking after it. He would be involved in expenses, of strong-rooms and guards to watch over them; so if the deposit was a commercial transaction, he would have to be paid for his services. If the deposit is looked at as a loan (and it is very like a loan) it carries negative interest. But that is not the way in which at first it is likely to be looked at.[1] It will not be looked at like that until custody has become a regular business.[2]

Then, once that happens, there will be a clear incentive to bring together the two activities—lending to the market, and 'borrowing' as custodian from the general public—for the second provides the funds which in the first are needed. At that point the combined concern will indeed have been becoming a bank.[3]

But it will not have quite got there even yet. For there is a further step, what looks like being a risky step, which it is almost bound to be tempted to take. The funds which had become available to it could be more, even much more, than it could use for its business on the bill market; why not look for other borrowers? Borrowers outside the bill market could not give that market's kinds of assurance; but surely there would be some who look like being reliable. We certainly find that the earliest banks, which merit that description, were doing at least some outside lending.[4]

So I shall, I hope acceptably, reckon a firm to be a bank, a fully formed bank, when it is doing all these things: (1) accepting deposits, (2) discounting bills, and (3) making advances to customers. I have tried to show how these could have come together. But what of the fourth function, commonly attributed to a bank, that of providing a medium of payment; how does that fit in? Let us see.

If a bank, as so far described, is to extend its business, it must increase its lending, in the one form or the other; and when it has

---

[1] The leading custodians, in ancient times, would probably have been temples, or other religious foundations. To put your treasure in the care of a god would have been a prime way of keeping it safe. But this would not be thought of as a commercial transaction. It would have been mixed up with outright gifts.

[2] It survives as such to the present day, as when a bank makes a charge for keeping a small account.

[3] Custody is sometimes described as 'cloak-room banking'. But it surely makes for clarity to regard it as no more than a step on the way to banking.

[4] I am thinking of early banks in Renaissance Italy.

exhausted the funds which have been entrusted to it for safe keeping (and any perhaps which are in its own possession) it cannot go further without increasing its deposits. Thus it has an incentive to encourage deposits. There are two main ways in which this can be done.

One is to offer a (positive) rate of interest on deposits. The interest it pays must be less than what it earns on advances, or it could not make a profit. Here the bank is acting as an intermediary on the loan market, between those who lend to it and those who borrow from it. This is expensive to the bank, but competition will often ensure that it has to be done.

The other is to make it easier for depositors to make use of the funds which they have deposited. They have been thinking that their deposits were available to be called upon when needed, characteristically to pay a debt. If this meant that cash (gold or silver) had to be taken out of the bank, and then posted to the creditor, the safe keeping (which was the purpose of the exercise) would be most imperfectly achieved, since the package could get lost or stolen on the way. It would however always have happened that when cash was deposited in the bank, some form of receipt would be given by the bank. If the receipt were made transferable, it could itself be used in payment of the debt, and that should be safer. But for this to become a general practice, the bank must co-operate. It must issue receipts in standard amounts (bank notes). It would indeed be necessary that the creditor should have confidence in the bank, so that he accepts the bank's promise to pay as being as good as money. There might at first be sufficient confidence for this only within a narrow circle.

Nevertheless, as time went on, the circle could widen. The bank notes could become a quasi-money, in rather general use. (Historically, when that point was reached, the government could begin to be interested, and could put restrictions on bank-note circulation.) Even apart from that, the more widely acceptable the bank notes are, the more tempting it is to steal them. So the bank-note device, intended as a protection, would defeat itself. A further protection was therefore required.

This was found in getting the bank itself to make the transfer—a device which in the end became payment by cheque. It would at first be necessary for the payer to give an order to his bank, then to notify the payee that he had done so, then for the payee to collect from the bank. Later it was discovered that so much correspondence was not needed. A single document, sent by debtor to creditor, instructing the creditor to collect from the bank, would suffice. It would be the bank's business to inform the creditor whether or not the instruction was accepted, whether (that is) the debtor had enough in his account in the bank to be able to pay. In most business dealings the debtor would have looked after that before drawing his cheque. But if he had overdrawn, the bank would inform both parties that the cheque was ineffective, so no payment had been made.

It is easy to see why this has become so common a way of making payments, at least in an economy where most people have bank accounts, for it is a superior way of minimizing transaction costs. But the consequences of its general adoption are notable. For it means that the whole of the bank deposits which are withdrawable at sight become usable as money. They are usable as such by the depositors in the bank, and—what is even more remarkable—they are usable as money by the bank itself. It is true that they are not a store of value for the bank, since they figure on the liabilities side of its balance-sheet, not on the assets side. But they can be used by the bank itself as a medium of payment.

When the bank makes a loan it hands over money, getting a statement of debt (bill, bond or other security) in return. The money might be taken from cash which the bank had been holding, and in the early days of banking that may often have happened. But it could be all the same to the borrower if what he received was a withdrawable deposit in the bank itself. The bank deposit is money from his point of view, so from his point of view there is nothing special about the transaction. But from the point of view of the bank, it has acquired the security, without giving up any cash; the counterpart, in its balance-sheet, is an increase in its liabilities. There is expansion, from its point of view, on each side of its balance-sheet. But from the point of view of the rest of the economy, the bank has 'created' money. This is not to be denied.

But before concluding at once, as many do, that this increase in the 'quantity of money' is inherently inflationary, or 'dis-deflationary', we should further examine the effect on the bank itself.

We have seen that the bank can be regarded as an intermediary, between those (depositors) who lend to it and those who borrow from it. The lenders are to be attracted by facility of withdrawal; but what corresponds to that on the borrowing side? An outside borrower, who wants money now, will usually[5] want it in order to spend it; but however profitably it is that he spends it, he cannot expect to be able to repay until some time has elapsed. Thus the bulk of the advances that are made by the bank will have to be for appreciable periods. The banker cannot expect to be able to recall his advances just when he wishes to do so. He may try to arrange them so that repayments are coming in fairly steadily; but that does not change the essential point that the money he has advanced will not come back until some date in the future, which he has accepted in the past but cannot now be changed.

If deposits are withdrawable on demand, or at short notice, while advances are relatively immovable, the position of the bank is inherently risky. It must always be exposed to some danger of a 'run'— many withdrawals coming together.

There seem to be three main ways in which a bank can protect itself against these risks, risks which are inherent in the kind of business it is doing.

One is to take advantage of the 'law of large numbers'. There must probably be something of this if banking, as a continuing business, is to function at all; but the protection which it offers does not by itself extend very far. For all that is said by this statistical principle, applied to banking, is that when a large number of similar transactions are being undertaken, in each of which there is a chance of some kind of failure, but the risk in one is independent of that in another, the loss that needs to be allowed for over the whole, when that is taken together, should be fairly predictable. This applies on both sides of the business of the bank. In the case of advances, failure consists in the borrower failing to repay at the appointed date; that can be looked after, on the statistical principle, by making a provision for bad debts. In the case of deposits, the risk that is undertaken by the banker is uncertainty of date of withdrawal; that also can be spread, if there are many depositors, and what makes one withdraw does not affect the behaviour of others. There have nevertheless been important cases when independence, on one side or the other, has been counted on but has failed. If the customers, who receive the advances, are most of them doing the same sort of business, when one is in trouble

---

[5] Usually, because in practice there is an exception. He may borrow, although he does not plan to spend until a later date, if he thinks he can get the money more easily, or on more favourable terms, than he would be able to get it later. I shall leave this aside for the present.

many others may be also; thus a bank which is specialized on lending to farmers, itself gets into trouble in an agricultural depression. Withdrawals by depositors, who have begun to suspect that the bank may not be able to pay, are very likely to be imitated by others. So on each side there are possible conditions when the statistical protection does not work.

A second way in which banks have commonly protected themselves is to avoid allowing too much of the funds entrusted to them to be tied up in advances. Some may be held in the form of cash; but even if no interest is being paid on deposits, to hold a money, which bears no interest, as corresponding asset is clearly unprofitable. Bills are obviously a better alternative; and something of the same advantage can be got on suitable occasions, from longer-dated securities also. They can be expected to be sellable in an emergency, though the price at which they can then be sold is uncertain.

A third recourse, which in modern times has become of major importance, is to borrow from another bank. If there exists a group of banks, which are prepared when called on to lend to one another, the group is stronger than any of its constituents would be by itself. Strength is needed; so a certain amount of association of this sort has an economic function. By those who stand for competition 'though the heavens fall' it is under suspicion; but the virtues of competition, in cases where failure has wide repercussions, are open to qualification. How far this dilemma is resolved by the creation of a Central Bank—in fact, even if not in name, a Government Bank—in which the monopoly element is concentrated, I shall be considering in Chapter 11.

It will be observed that of these three protections, it is only the second which has the quality that the extent to which it is used can be continuously under the control of the bank itself. To get a loan from another bank requires the consent of that other bank; to vary the independencies, or interdependencies, between the risks involved in its advances, or in its deposits, can only be matter of long-term policy. But it is open to the bank at any moment to vary the size of its cash holdings, by buying or selling securities. It is therefore inevitable that operation upon this margin should be central to the management of the bank.

It is true that its advances will be 'rolling over'; some, at any time, will be being repaid, and (normally) being replaced by new advances, or continuations. Thus one way in which a bank may replenish its cash holdings is by cutting down on replacements. But the most that can be got from this source, at all quickly, will be limited. Advances are not so liquid as investments (in securities) are.

So this is where we come to the concept of *liquidity*, and here we have it in the banking context where it first appeared in the work of Keynes.[6] Bankers, he told us in his *Treatise*, have

three categories [of assets] to choose from: (1) bills of exchange and call loans to the money market, (2) investments, and (3) advances to customers. As a rule, advances to customers are more profitable than investments, and investments are more profitable than bills and call loans; but that order is not invariable. On the other hand, bills and call loans are more *liquid* than investments, i.e. more certainly realizable at short notice without loss, and investments are more liquid than advances.

I regard this passage as extremely important, not merely because it is the first place where Keynes spoke of liquidity (and it may also be the first place where any economic or financial writer spoke of liquidity[7]) but also because it is better than the simplified version of which Keynes himself made use in his later work. But it has not had the impact it deserved, for it needs some explanation and working-out.

First, explanations. 'Realizable' means convertible into cash, or money; but why money? Because it is in money that its liabilities—particularly its sight liabilities, deposits withdrawable on demand—are expressed.[8] Thus cash, that is held among its assets, would seem to be treatable as perfectly liquid. Advances we have been reckoning not to be cashable at all 'at short notice'. Thus until the time for repayment comes, they are completely illiquid; their liquidity is zero. Degrees of liquidity can only pertain, in the case of the bank, to the securities segment of its assets (bills, bonds or maybe equities). It is only these which can be *more or less liquid*.

When liquidity is defined in this manner, it becomes clear that it is

---

[6] *Treatise on Money*, Volume 2, p. 67.

[7] I maintained this priority, in a paper entitled *Liquidity*, published in the *Economic Journal* (1962) and reprinted in my *Collected Essays*, Volume II (1983), pp. 238–47. It is difficult to prove it. I can only claim that I looked for it in a number of writings of the twenties, where it would have been appropriate for the writer to have used it, and did not find it. No one has told me I was wrong.

[8] If there is more than one sort of money in which its liabilities are expressed, such as its 'own' money and a foreign money, and there is no fixed rate of exchange between them, things become more complicated. I shall have a little to say about that very contemporary problem later (see Chapter 14).

a *quality* which is attributed to an asset, according to a judgement that is made by its proprietor, or by some other interested party, at a particular moment. The 'loss', of which the definition speaks, must be the difference between the current market price of the asset and what it might fetch if it were to be disposed of at an unfavourable moment. (The need for such disposal might arise on the liabilities side, such as on withdrawal of deposits, or on the asset side, for example a new opportunity for profitable lending in the form of advances.) Just when it would be desired to make such a disposal is unknown.

Let us now look again, in the light of these considerations, at the balance-sheet of the bank. Its 'investments' we are now to reckon as 'more or less liquid'; its advances as nearly illiquid (at least so far as the near future is concerned); its holding of cash, on the principle just explained, as perfectly liquid; but is that right? Most, and sometimes even all, of its cash is normally employed on its regular business, covering gaps between deposits and withdrawals; these go on all the time, without creating any 'emergency'. It needs to have a money holding for this purpose, but this is *not* a liquid asset, from the bank's point of view. When this is allowed for, we ought to say that liquidity is a characteristic of an asset that is held *as a reserve*. The money that is held for current transactions is not a reserve asset; it is what corresponds to the working capital of a manufacturing business. I find it convenient to call this a *running asset*. (Advances also, when it is expected that they will go on being replaced, or renewed, are in this sense a running asset.)

In these terms, it can readily be seen what we should mean by the liquidity of the balance-sheet as a whole. It must be a matter of the quantity, and quality, of the reserves. This must be measured against possible calls on those reserves, which are essentially a matter of withdrawal of deposits. So it is tempting to say that the liquidity of the bank should be measured by the ratio of its reserves to its deposits. If there are advances, so that not all deposits are covered by reserves, then on this measure the bank is always imperfectly liquid.

But liquidity is a matter of quality as well as quantity. Among the reserves there will be some which have high liquidity, some (perhaps) very much less. They shade into one another. So though it is true that banking liquidity is a matter of comparison between reserves and deposits, it is not a comparison that can readily be reduced to an arithmetical ratio. For the liquidity index which is to be attached to a particular security will vary over time and over state of mind—even the state of mind of the market as a whole.

It is nevertheless understandable that people who make decisions about liquidity (and people, such as economists, who think about people making those decisions) should want to work in such terms as can be put into an arithmetical form. If the 'more or less' liquid assets could be shepherded into two classes, on the one hand those that are very liquid, and on the other those that are decidedly illiquid, an arithmetical comparison between the very liquid and the deposits would serve as a good proxy for liquidity in general. But such a separation may not be easy to make, or to maintain. The best place for making it may shift from one time to another.

This has a bearing on what has happened to one part of the economics of Keynes. I have been greatly helped in this chapter by what he said on liquidity in his *Treatise*; but in his later and more famous book he seems to have fallen into the trap just described. And how many of his monetarist followers—in this respect they were his followers!—he led into it. One can see how it happened. During the years 1932–8 (just when Keynes was writing his *General Theory* and defending it against its first critics) the market rate of discount on bills, in London, was hardly more than one-half per cent. So bills were standing at a discount which was practically negligible; to treat them as *being* money, as Keynes implicitly did, was very natural. If bills were money, there was just one margin to be considered, among the reserves of a bank (or other financier): that between money so extended and other investments (bonds). So he could show his *long-term* rate of interest being determined at that margin. But this was a state of affairs which did not persist; from the perspective of fifty years later it appears an aberration. As things have been since the 1950s, not only in Britain but in other countries, short rates have been much higher, and there have been numerous issues with medium maturities, by governments and others, all the way between the bills of Keynes's time and his long-term bonds, or the nearest to the latter which still exist. Where, in this continuum, do we draw a line? it is no wonder that there has been such a fuss about the sorts of claims that are to be reckoned as money, M_x and M_y and so on! In what has become the modern world, there can be no answer to that question. We have to go back to the qualitative concept of the *Treatise*.

And it is not only for theory of banking that we need it. I shall be looking at it in a wider way in the chapter which follows.

8 Choice among Assets

It was rather obvious that the liquidity concept, which in Keynes's *Treatise* (1930)—in the passage quoted in the previous chapter—had been confined in application to the behaviour of banks, could be reinterpreted so as to give it a wider reference. Any sort of financial firm would be confronted with similar alternatives, and so could have assets of various degrees of liquidity. One could think of it being faced with a 'spectrum' of such assets from which to choose, a spectrum which could be wider or narrower than that on which a bank would usually work. And having gone so far, why not go further? Why not look for liquidity elements in the decisions of all sorts of firms, and even in the management of his property by the private capitalist? So there were two directions in which the concept might be generalized—to the decisions of more sorts of choosers and between more sorts of assets.

This generalization was not made in Keynes's *General Theory* (1936); the generality from which that took its title was in a different direction. The *Treatise* had been a theory of the influence of money on *prices*; its analysis was extended, or transformed, in the later work, to the influence of money on activity of production also. Nothing like that happened on the side of liquidity. His new *Liquidity Preference* theory was another special case, where choice is restricted to two assets, money and securities; the latter being interpreted sometimes as long-term bonds, sometimes as something which is to stand for securities in general. So Liquidity Preference became a theory of *the* rate of interest. Differences in liquidity between different securities, on which attention was concentrated in the *Treatise* definition, have disappeared from sight. (I have explained the historical circumstances which could have led Keynes to suppose that this procedure was sufficient.)

Nearly a year before the appearance of the *General Theory* I had myself published (in *Economica*, February 1935) my 'Suggestion for simplifying the theory of money'. This, though it does not use the word *liquidity*, was a step in the direction of what was required. I think it has become quite widely accepted that this is so. It was stated that the theory should apply to any decision-maker; the spectrum on which he operates is drawn very wide, extending from money at one end, through more or less liquid securities, to real capital goods at the other. I am still quite happy with that way of formulating the problem. There does not seem to be much that is wrong with what I said about it.[1]

Nevertheless there is something which ought to have been there but is missing. It is something which is in Keynes (of 1936); that of course at the time I was writing was not at my disposal. It is his famous classification of motives for holding money—his transactions, precautionary and speculative motives—which should have found a place. It could have been generalized in just the way I was generalizing; but it was not until many years later[2] that I saw how that was to be done. It can now very usefully be made to fit.

Keynes's *motives* were purposes for which money may be held. The step which had to be taken, corresponding to that taken in my 'Suggestion', was to notice that money is only one of the assets that may be held for corresponding purposes. We have already seen, in the case of the bank, that its cash may be a running asset (corresponding to Keynes's transaction motive) or it may be a reserve asset (corresponding to his precautionary); also that, in the case of the bank, there are other assets which may be held for just these purposes. It is possible, in the case of the bank, that these two may exhaust all the purposes for which assets are held; for its advances, if they are turning over regularly, would count as running assets. For a bank to be holding cash for a speculative motive must, as we shall see, be uncommon. But there clearly is another purpose, not so far classified, for which assets may be held—just to get an income from them—as a private capitalist, to take the most obvious example, may hold a portfolio of securities. It has not been easy to find a good name for this third category of assets. The private capitalist calls them his 'investments'; so it probably gives the right impression to call them 'investment assets'. That has been my usual practice, which I shall here maintain. I am however by no means entirely satisfied with it.[3]

---

[1] As the spectrum was written out in my 'Suggestion', consumption goods appear at the more liquid end! This was clearly a mistake.

[2] First in the third of 'Two triads' (*Critical Essays*, 1967). A later version is 'Solidity, fluidity and liquidity', a new paper put into the second volume of my *Collected Essays* (1983). I am still quite satisfied with nearly the whole of the latter, so I shall not abstain from quoting quite a lot of it verbatim.

[3] It does not fit the usage of the *Treatise*, where the bank is reckoning what clearly are reserve assets as 'investments'.

Some kinds of assets are financial claims; others are property rights in real goods. This is a different classification from that we have been making, but both are needed. So what results is a six-way table:

	Running	Reserve	Investment
Real	A	B	C
Financial	D	E	F

What kinds of asset should we put into each of these boxes? Let us look for some examples.

We should not expect that in every balance-sheet there would be instances of all six. A manufacturing firm will have real running assets (A) in the form of goods in process, and of plant and machinery in use. They are running assets because they are in active use, in the work on which the firm is engaged. It will probably have some real reserve assets (B) in the form of reserve stocks of materials, and perhaps some equipment, machines and suchlike, which will only come into use in the event of a need for repairs, or some similar emergency. It is not easy to see that there is a need for such a firm to have real investment assets (C). But there are other entities which clearly have them. An obvious case, to the present writer, is the land which is held by some Oxford and Cambridge colleges *as an investment*. Land-holding is not the regular business of the college; the land is just held to get an income from it.

Real assets (B) that are held as reserves are already embodied in specific forms, so they are only usable as reserves in suitable emergencies. But the kinds of emergency that may arise can never be exactly foreseen; so a form of reserve that is not so tied down must in general be required. This is the function of the financial reserve assets (E) which we should thus expect to be very widely held. One is indeed tempted to say that any business, which is not to be in danger of collapse, must have some financial reserves. But this does not necessarily mean that it must have these reserves as assets, for there is a possible alternative. As we saw in the case of the banks themselves, assured borrowing power, probably from a bank, will do as a substitute. This may take the form of an agreed overdraft, but it need not be so formal. We may perhaps reckon it as an 'invisible asset'. It does not appear on a company balance-sheet, in the form in which that is published; it is one of the reasons why the balance-sheet needs to be 'annotated' if it is to be properly informative. The corresponding item in the balance-sheet of the bank is an 'invisible liability'.

Financial investment assets (F) have already been mentioned, as a principal asset of the private capitalist—or of the pension fund or charitable trust. It is an essential characteristic of the assets in this compartment that they are held for their yield, for the interest or dividends that are to be derived from them.

There remain the financial running assets (D) which are clearly of major importance for monetary theory. For money, in some sense or other, in the till, in the pocket or in the bank account, is without doubt a leading financial running asset, for almost any entity. Indeed there must be many for which it is the only item under D. If a firm has non-money items under D we should probably reckon it to be to some degree a dealer in money—a financial firm.

Nothing has been said directly so far about the *speculative* motive of Keynes. If (as Keynes often did) we regard it as an essential characteristic of money that it does not bear interest, it would seem at first sight that no money should be held under F. For these assets are held for their yield, for the income that is expected to be derived from them. Keynes nevertheless maintained that money could be held under F for his speculative motive. This was quite a shock to some of his first readers, who had been thinking that an investor, who bought a security in order to derive an income from it, would be intending to hold it indefinitely. If he had that intention, there would be no point in holding 'barren money'. Keynes however was not thinking of that sort of investor, but of one who plans to *manage his portfolio*, selling and buying again as opportunity offers. There can surely be no question, when one faces the issue, that both types are types which occur. We shall need to have names for them; suitable names have already come to hand in the context of the labour market in Chapter 4. So I shall say that the one type invests *solid*, the other *fluid*.

There can be no doubt that there will be occasions when a fluid investor will act as a bear speculator. If he expects a fall in the prices of securities (a rise in rates of interest) he will sell and then, if his expectation is correct, buy back at a lower price. During the interval he will have held his funds idle, for a speculative motive. Even if he gets no interest on the funds held idle during the interval, he still makes a gain, over the transaction as a whole. Nor is it true, as some of Keynes's critics objected, that the gain is a capital gain while the loss is an income loss; and that they are incommensurable. It is only by tax legislation that they have been made incommensurable; otherwise they are commensurable.

Suppose it is expected that the rate of interest on a (long-term) bond will rise, from 4 to 5 per cent, within a year. The sum of £100 invested now will yield £4 per annum; if invested later, it looks like yielding £5 per annum; thus by delay there is a gain of £1 per annum, in perpetuity, against a loss of £4, at the most, during the period of delay. Considered purely in income terms this is a very profitable investment. The barren money, properly accounted for, is not without yield. So one must accept that there is this case when money may be held as an investment asset. Nevertheless, though so much attention has been paid to it, this is not the chief way in which the solidity–fluidity distinction is important.

The general liquidity theory, of which a first sketch was given in my 'Suggestion', gains greatly in force when attention is paid to it.

A solid investor, though he may choose his investment with care at the moment when he makes it, can only do so in the light of what he knows at that moment. He denies himself the opportunity of changing his decision, in the light of further information available later. The fluid investor is not denied that opportunity; this to him is an advantage. Why should the former deny himself that advantage? The obvious answer is transaction costs. Every act of investment (and disinvestment) in securities ordinarily involves some costs— which may be subjective, the time and trouble involved, but may also be quite objective, brokerage charges in particular. If a portfolio is managed in a very fluid manner, these transaction costs must pile up. They have to be deducted from the gains from fluidity if there is to be a net advantage of changing over to a fluid policy. It is therefore of the first importance that there are likely to be great differences in the transaction costs that are faced by investors of different sorts.

One can assert with some confidence that transaction costs, of most kinds, increase less than proportionally to the volume of funds to be invested, at least for large differences in volume. This is shown, if it needs showing, by the fact that when the portfolio is large, it pays to have specialized departments, or equivalent organizations, to do the managing; it does not pay when the portfolio is smaller. Thus it is essentially the large investor who can profitably pursue a fluid policy; it does not pay the small investor to do so. It is better for him to invest at least fairly solid.

This indeed implies that he is investing for income, that what he is buying is to be an investment asset under F. For his reserve assets he is more in the position of a bank—in which, in practice, most of his

reserve is likely to be deposited. Reserve funds are held against emergencies, whose extent and time of occurrence are not exactly foreseen. If the date of requirement is completely uncertain—it may just
as well be in the near future as further ahead—it will be essential
that the funds should be held in a form which makes them realizable
easily, at any moment. And this does not only mean that they must
be held in securities that are readily marketable; it also means that
the value of the portfolio held for this purpose is not likely to vary too
much over time. So they must, in the sense of the *Treatise* definition,
be at least fairly liquid assets.

Banking itself, from this point of view, can be regarded as a device
by which outsiders (outside the financial sector) can obtain the
liquidity they require by using the bank as an intermediary. Both by
operating on a larger scale and by being more professional, banks
reduce transaction costs—and so can, at least in principle, operate
more efficiently. From the point of view of the depositor, there is a
substitute for the transaction cost, which he would otherwise have to
bear himself, in a price for its service which he pays to the bank.

So it can be also with respect to investment assets (F). Here also
there is an opportunity for an intermediary.

It is true that the manager of a pure investment fund does not have
to attend to the value of his portfolio, as it may be in the event of
some external emergency, arising at an uncertain date, as the
manager of a reserve fund has to do. But he also needs to be in a position to be able to take advantage of opportunities for profitable
investment, which may arise in the future but cannot now be foreseen. If he is illiquid, being tied up in securities, the value of which at
an uncertain future date is uncertain, he may find that an opportunity arises, just when the value of his portfolio is abnormally low. He
can then expect to make a (capital) gain just from staying where he
is; that which is promised by the new opportunity must be greater
than this if it is to be acceptable. So he will often have to let it pass.

For this reason, and for the more obvious reason—especially important in the case of investment in equities, and in foreign securities
affected by rates of exchange—that new information about the prospect of particular securities is continually forthcoming, also by the
manager of an investment fund (F) there is something to be gained
from operating in a fluid manner. Even the small saver, who is saving
to buy himself an income for his retirement, or to leave to his depend-
ants, would gain from fluidity, if he could afford it. If he has no choice

but to invest in securities directly, not being able to afford fluidity, it is better for him to make his choice and stick to it, thus investing solid. He may nevertheless be able to gain some of the advantages of fluidity, by using an intermediary—by depositing or buying shares in an intermediary, such as an investment trust. Modern financial systems are rich in such devices; so it may seem at first sight as if solid investment, except by institutions that are legally bound to it, must be on the way to disappearing. It is for instance well known that the proportion of the value of all securities, traded on the London Stock Exchange, that is held directly by private people has for long been diminishing. But does this mean that the economist can take it for granted that an assumption of perfect fluidity is good enough for his purposes? I think one can show that this is not the case.

I have insisted (following the *Treatise*) that liquidity, applied to the securities sector of a balance-sheet, is a relative concept; money indeed may be taken to be perfectly liquid (because it is the standard in which debts are reckoned), other securities however only more or less. Should not something similar be true of our solidity and fluidity? Perfect solidity raises no problems; perfect fluidity is what we appear to have just encountered; but have we any right to it? As we shall find in the next chapter, it is an instructive hypothesis for some purely theoretical models; but is it more than that? I do not think it is.

The formal reason is that time is continuous. However short-sighted speculators may be, however negligible their transaction costs, they are always speculating with an eye to the future, a future which is surely always some finite distance away. It is not good enough to say that tomorrow is future, while today is present; for that leaves room for an active speculation on differences between morning and afternoon. However short we make the 'horizon', room can always be found for something shorter. It should further be remembered that our transaction costs are partly subjective; even if objective costs are negligible, there must surely be some of those operating on the market who would prefer not to have to give their decision-making sleepless attention.

I accept that modern 'financial innovation' has given stock markets great fluidity. But if that fluidity was perfect—certainly if it was always perfect—they would not work in the way we find them doing. A bull market might go on creeping upwards, with fluid investors continually making profits, until it had reached a level which anyone with a longer horizon could see straight off was just silly. But as long as there was a balance of optimist buyers over pessimist sellers it could go on rising; it would not turn until the balance turned the other way. All that is consistent with perfect fluidity. It is also consistent with perfect fluidity that the fall, once it came, should be sharp. For everyone would be trying to get out at once. As long as such fluidity remained dominant, the fall would continue. It must continue, under perfect fluidity, until all the securities traded had become waste paper. But even in the most free and most sophisticated market, that does not happen.

What stops it, without any 'intervention', is that some of the dealers (granted that they are professional dealers) start to look further forward, and discover that they can make a very reliable profit just by holding on. They introduce, in doing so, a little solidity. It is not enough to prevent the market being very unstable, but it is enough to prevent complete collapse. It is against this background that the monetary policy, which I shall be considering in later chapters, should be thought of as in principle operating.

9 Theories of Interest:
Keynes versus Marshall

To choose Marshall as leading opponent of Keynes on interest may seem peculiar, for Marshall had died a whole decade before Liquidity Preference came into the world. I have nevertheless come to feel sure that when Keynes spoke of 'classical' theory it was Marshall's he had in mind. He had learned and then taught in the school of economics that Marshall had founded at Cambridge; it was the doctrine that he himself had been teaching that he was now deliberately casting off.

This was not easily understood by those who did not have that background. They supposed a 'classic' to mean any earlier influential economist who was a stranger to Keynes's innovations. This indeed is the interpretation which has largely survived.[1] But by writing down the part of Marshall in the story something, as we shall see, has been lost.

It can be recovered once we recognize that there was an aspect of the 'revolution' which was internal to Cambridge. It led to a split in the Cambridge school. There were some of the Cambridge economists who followed Keynes; but there were others, of whom Robertson was the most persistent, who remained faithful to Marshall.[2] They did

---

[1] A footnote is the proper place for my personal part in the story. I have to admit that I am myself responsible for some of the misinterpretation. My 'Mr Keynes and the classics' was published in *Econometrica* in 1937; it was written for econometrists who were no Marshallians. So it was that when Keynes saw it, though he found my version of his own theory fairly acceptable (it is what has later become known as the ISLM diagram), he insisted that I had got the 'classics' all wrong. My 'classical' was much more primitive than his 'classical' theory. I now regard this as evidence that his 'classic' was Marshall. Though when I wrote that piece I had been teaching for some months in Cambridge, I was not acclimatized to Cambridge; my background was still what I had learned in my years at LSE. As it turned out, there were many economists, not only econometrists, who were in much the same position as I was, so what I said went down well with them. It has gone on going well.

[2] I was a close friend of Robertson's, so we had many discussions together; but never in his lifetime (he died in 1963) did we get the matter straight. The first step forward, in my own thinking, came in the writing of the chapters on stocks and flows in my *Capital and Growth* (1965). But it was only as a result of discussions with that fervent Robertsonian, Professor S. C. Tsiang, that I was impelled to make the effort to go over the old ground again. A first sketch of what I shall be saying here was pre-

have something to say; but they could have put it more convincingly if they had put it in the form of saying that there was something significant in Marshall that had not survived in Keynes. (They could then have admitted that the same might be true the other way.) That is what in this chapter I shall try to show.

The formal difference between Keynes's theory and that of the others is that Keynes looked at stocks—what is needed, at a particular moment, for a given stock of bonds to be held—while the others looked at flows, of borrowing and lending, over a period. It will be useful to begin with the simplest possible model in which the issue comes up.

This is a model of a closed economy, in which there are just two things which are exchangeable for money—one being goods (including services), the other bonds, which are (reliable) promises to pay a regular income, fixed in money terms, to whoever is the holder. The bonds are homogeneous, and we can make the goods homogeneous, by supposing that their *relative* prices are fixed exogenously. So there are just two prices to be determined, the price of goods and the price of bonds, the latter being (arithmetically) expressible as a rate of interest.

So as to give the flow aspect due attention, let us consider the working of the model during a period. A period must have a start and it must have a finish. If we consider the start by itself, we must look at stocks. There will be in this initial position, a certain stock of bonds and a certain stock of money. The price of the bond must be such that there are holders who taken together are willing to hold that particular stock of bonds, neither more nor less. A change in their holdings of bonds must, in the first place, imply a purchase or sale of bonds for money. So if we just look at that by itself, it is a change which must be effected by people who have a choice between holding money or holding bonds. The clearest case in which there is such a choice is when the holding of money and the holding of bonds are directed to much the same purpose; and it is hard to see that this can be anything else but that which figures in Keynes's theory, a requirement for liquidity, for a reserve against emergencies.

It thus appears that if we just look at the start of the period, what

sented to a conference, organized by him, at Taipei, Taiwan, at the end of 1985. Through collaboration with him I think I have found a plank, by which the stream can at last be crossed.

happens then must be determined by stock relations, which lead to Liquidity Preference in Keynes's manner. But the flow party will rightly say that we must not stop at that point; we must go on to see what happens during the period.

The period indeed has a finish as well as a start; and there seems to be no reason why the finish, if taken by itself, should not be treated in the same way as appeared to be appropriate for the start. But the *difference* between the position at the end, from what it was at the beginning, must be a matter of what has happened during the period. If new bonds have been issued during the period, the stock of bonds at the end must be different from what it was at the beginning. The *change* in the rate of interest during the period must then be a matter of what is needed for this additional stock to be held.

It would have to be said by a thoroughgoing Keynesian theorist that these extra bonds would have to be taken up by people who were willing to add them to their reserves, holding them as a substitute for money reserves which they would otherwise have been holding. Thus, unless there were new supplies of money coming in, from outside, during the period, the change in the rate of interest would be a matter of the elasticity of a Liquidity Preference curve.

A quite consistent stock-flow theory could be constructed on those lines; but I think it is clear that a good Marshallian, such as Robertson, would have refused to accept it. For he would have refused to accept that the holding of bonds *as a reserve asset* is the only reason for holding bonds.

I have myself insisted (in the previous chapter) that there is another reason for holding them; they may be held as *investment* assets, just to get a regular income from them. Surely it is this which the bond, which here we are postulating, most obviously promises.

If one is just looking at the (initial) stock equilibrium, the introduction of this 'investment' motive is a little awkward; so one sees how it was possible for Keynesians to leave it out. But when one passes to the question of the rate of interest which can be maintained over a period, it must come into place. For it cannot then be denied that extra bonds might be held, not as reserve assets, but as sources of income, accumulated out of savings. If the new bonds, issued during the period, were matched by new savings, made during the period, there need be no additional bonds to be held by those who were holding them as a reserve. The level of the rate of interest could then remain unchanged over the period. Equality between 'saving' and 'investment' would allow it to remain unchanged, and would allow the supply and demand for 'goods' to remain in balance.

A model in which all these things were taken into account could not I think have failed of acceptance, at least in principle, both by Robertson and by Keynes. But, having got so far in agreement, they would still have had their differences. These would not have been theoretical differences, in a narrow sense; they would have been differences of judgement on which of the choice margins that had been identified were of practical importance. This, being an empirical question, could have been answered, quite properly, in different ways at different times. It could be that it would have been proper to answer it in one way in the 1880s (Marshall), in another in the 1920s and 1930s (Keynes and Robertson), in another in the 1980s, to which we have come. And maybe to answer it in different ways in different countries.

To deal at all adequately with the historical questions which thus come into sight would require research, for which I do not have facility. There are nevertheless a few facts which are available to me, from which it might begin.

Any British economist, at the time of Marshall, would have thought that he knew what the pure long-term rate of interest was; it was the yield on consols. Consols (market jargon for consolidated stock) already had a history. It had been as long ago as 1752 that the National Debt of the British Government, which in the first half-century of its existence had been largely owed to a few big corporations (Bank of England, East India Company, and so on) had been converted into this single transferable stock which became known as consols. Information about the price of consols (and hence about the long-term interest rate) from that date to his could have been available to Marshall. One may surely suppose that he would have had at least some idea about it.

The nominal rate of interest on consols, for nearly all that time, had been 3 per cent. The holder could not demand repayment, though he could sell his stock on the market; but the Government had the right to repay at par, if it was in a position to do so. That came to mean, in practice, if it could reborrow at less than 3 per cent. That never happened until the time of Marshall, when in 1888 there was a conversion, the Goschen conversion, to $2\frac{1}{2}$ per cent.

We happen to know what Marshall thought about that conversion—or rather about the fall in interest rates which preceded it, for the conversion was announced in the budget speech in March, and Marshall's statement was in the preceding December.[3] It will be useful to quote it, though it is more flamboyant than is usual with Marshall, since it shows the context in which he looked at his theory:

> It seems to me that the great economic feature of this age, more important than every other fact put together, is that the amount of capital is increasing many times as fast as that of population. It is increasing faster than ever in England and, what is much more important, there is a very rapid increase in America where everyone almost is saving. The 'extravagant' American is saving more than any other person. In spite of the inventions which are continually making new uses for capital in the form of machinery and in other ways, this vast increase forces down the interest that can be got in business. The rate of discount, in my opinion, is merely the ripple of a wave on the surface. The average level is the rate of interest which can be got from the investment of capital, and this is being lowered by the rapid and steady growth of capital—I do not mean the growth of credit, I mean the growth of things, the actual excess of production over consumption. I do not see any necessity at all why interest should be more than 2 per cent a century hence. I should not be surprised at all if a railway company could borrow on debentures at 2, or even less than 2 per cent, in the next century.

So that was where the 'euthanasia of the rentier' came from. Keynes got it from Marshall!

Marshall, when he made that statement, knew that interest rates had been falling, and that for some time the 'three per cents' had been standing above par. But what could he have known about the flow of savings? The National Income statisticians, who were to give a later generation some information about that, had hardly yet been born. But he was not just guessing; he was deducing his 'fact' from his theory. Interest had been falling; so saving *must* have risen.

But how could he have explained, on his theory, what had happened further back? The financial history of the first quarter of his century would not have troubled him. Heavy borrowing during the Napoleonic War, with high rates of interest accompanying it; a surviving problem of debt, after the war, so alarming that Ricardo considered dealing with it by a capital levy; its successful absorption in the twenty years after Waterloo; all of that he could understand. But what of experience between the thirties and seventies?

---

[3] It was given as evidence to a public enquiry into monetary policy (Gold and Silver Commission). It is reprinted in the collection of Marshall's *Official Papers* (1926), p. 46. I owe the reference, of course, to Dennis Robertson.

During all that time there was great stability in the rate of interest (or yield on consols); it hardly moved outside the range of 3 to $3\frac{1}{2}$ per cent. There was very little government borrowing; but there was massive borrowing by railway companies, some of whose obligations, as Marshall recognized, were taken to be 'gilt-edged'. It would be to these that the 'flow of savings' would be largely directed. But why should flow demands and supplies of savings, over all these securities, have been so nearly in balance?

It is hard to find an explanation entirely on Marshall lines. Keynes's 'speculative motive' gives more help. It could be that already at this date an appreciable part of the stock of consols would be in the hands of professionals, who would be holding it *fluid*,[4] ready to buy or sell in pursuit of short-term gains. Consider the position of such a dealer, at some date in the middle of the century, consols standing at (say) 95. The maximum capital gain which he could expect from holding on would be relatively small; for if the price went above 100 there would be a threat of conversion. The maximum loss, on the other hand, might appear to be quite large. If possible gain and possible loss were to balance, the chance of a large loss must have been thought to be quite small. Why should that have been so?

It is not the case that during those years the British financial system, as a whole, as so stable. There were crises, of marked cyclical character, and of considerable severity (see Chapter 11). In those years there would be large movements of short-term rates on the money market (going up to 7 per cent in 1867). But their effect on the price of consols was remarkably small. Why should that have been so?

It would be enough if no one expected the crisis short rates to last long, if they were just taken to be 'ripples on the surface' as Marshall said. If the price of consols had been standing at 95, and was confidently expected to come back to that level in a few months, a fall of a point or two in the current price would offer a capital gain from hold-

---

[4] I have a bit of evidence for that, derived from Goschen himself. In the budget debate in the House of Commons, which followed upon the conversion, he was being attacked by an ignoramus on the Opposition side, who said the whole thing was what would later have been called a 'bankers' ramp'. Widows and orphans were being exploited for the benefit of bankers. Goschen replied that the bankers also were going to be hit, for a lot of the debt was already in their hands (A. D. Elliot, *Life of Goschen*, 1911, Volume 2, p. 153). It should be noted that Goschen had been a 'city man' before he went into politics.

ing which would balance a quite high short rate *for that time.* This would make little impression on the course, over years, of the long rate of interest.

Nevertheless, when we come to the fall in the long rate in the seventies and eighties, there is more to be said for Marshall. These were years of retarded growth (in Britain); the railway boom was ending; so a fall in the demand for savings (much more plausibly than an increase in supply) could well have been responsible for a fall in interest. It is true that the fall can, at least at first sight, be explained the other way. Over the twenty years before the Goschen conversion there had been no important commercial crises, so there was less danger of high short rates affecting long rates, even temporarily. (This also would have been a consequence of the retardation.) In a former discussion of the matter I gave much weight to this alternative.[5] but it is my present opinion that it does not get the time-sequence right. For surely the fall in interest rates is recognizable *before* this greater stability could have been recognized. So I now think that Marshall, after all, does win that trick in the game.

Keynes, in the 1930s, had all Marshall's experience behind him; and that of another forty years to add. The immediate problem with which he was confronted was more like Ricardo's than like Marshall's: another great war debt, but this time with international complications which in Ricardo's case had been absent. We know of the work he did in the twenties to find ways of escaping from those entanglements. By the time he came to write his *General Theory,* he could think of that task as being done. So his book, on the whole, is a theory of a closed economy.

Monetary measures, to match the 'absorption' of 1815–35, had already when he wrote been taken; the way for them had been cleared by the floating of the pound in 1931. There had then been a conversion, reducing the effective rate on (long) war debt from 5 per cent to $3\frac{1}{2}$ or thereabouts—more or less to the rate which had so long been held steady in the reign of Victoria. The practical problem, as Keynes saw it at the time he was writing, was to keep the (long) rate at the level it had so recently reached—to stop it going back to where it had been not so long ago. That he knew would be easier if the market could become convinced that $3\frac{1}{2}$ (or whatever it was) was the proper or normal rate—a rate which had some prestige. History

[5] *Critical Essays*, p. 93.

could give it some prestige, but that was a long time ago, So to restore its authority it would have to be maintained, for a considerable time; the market would have to get used to it. Then it might (perhaps) be put back, on to its throne.

Not enough time was in fact allowed for this experiment. The British economy, in 1936, was not starting on a long period of peace, with an old-fashioned Conservative government; quite the reverse. So it was not until the Second World War was over, when Keynes was no longer available as an adviser, that there seemed, to some people, to be another chance. I much doubt if Keynes would have thought or ought to have thought it to be another chance. Surely, on his principles, the 'Daltons' of 1947 came much too soon.

Looking back on all this from our own standpoint, with another forty years of experience at our disposal, there is surely one thing about it which stands out. In the days of Marshall, widely considered, and in those of Keynes, also widely considered, it was rates of interest between 2 and 5 per cent, at the extremes, which were being considered. Since 1950 we have become adjusted to rates which are at the least double. We are getting to think of 8 per cent as a very moderate rate; not, as it would have been in the old days, catastrophic. Why has this happened? This is the very topical question to which my historical enquiry has been leading up.

It is commonly thought that these high rates of interest are a consequence of inflation; that if prices are rising, at 4 per cent per annum, a nominal rate of interest of 8 per cent per annum is equivalent to a *real* rate of 4. It is true that inflation makes these high rates of interest bearable, so that their consequences are not so desperate as they would have been in the past. But to make those consequences into causes surely takes things the wrong way round. Does not Marshall come to the rescue? He would have attributed the high rates of interest to the great expansion of government expenditure, *in many countries*, for peace-time indeed rather than war-time purposes; and to the unwillingness of governments to impose the taxes to pay for them. That, he would have said, was how the phenomenon started; the high rates and the inflation were consequences of it; admittedly they facilitated each other. Would he have been wrong?

10 Markets in Equities: Ownership and Control

There is a curious correspondence between the matters to be considered in this chapter and those which were considered in Chapter 4 at the end of the first part of this book. We there saw that in the labour market there would be two sorts of employment to be distinguished, one of what I called established labour, where employer and employed expect their relation to continue for some time to come, and one in which there is no such expectation of continuance. There are advantages, from the point of view of economic efficiency, which either may have over the other. There are things which can be done by a team of people who are accustomed to working together, quickly understanding one another, which cannot be done by a collection of people more loosely attached. But the other has the advantage of being more easily adaptable. We should expect the typical firm to pay some attention to each of these advantages. It would then tend to employ a *nucleus* of established labour, to which a *fringe* of less established labour would be attached. Something like that would serve as a model of a typical firm.

Now surely in such a model the management itself would be included in the nucleus. So contracts between the managers, like those between themselves and their established employees, would be links which tie the firm together. If the managers are also proprietors, contracts between them in that capacity could also be regarded as linkages, of course important linkages. They would be expressed in terms of shares which particular proprietors hold.

A firm in which proprietors are also managers, and there are no other proprietors, can hardly be other than quite a small firm; whatever be the legal form that is given to it, it is economically a partnership. Shares in a partnership can, on occasion, be bought and sold. For one of the partners may retire from the business; he is 'bought out'; he sells his share to the others. But this will surely be a complicated transaction, requiring much negotiation; there can be no market, certainly no competitive market, for shares of that type. In order that there be such a market, the link between proprietorship

and management must be broken, or at least diluted. It was the institution of *Limited Liability* which brought this about.

In the absence of this facility, each partner would be personally
liable for the debts of the partnership; thus if a creditor could not
recover from it as a body, he could endeavour to recover from each of
them individually, against the whole of his assets, whether those
assets were engaged in the business or not. For the law would treat
his dealings through the firm as being done in his private capacity. It
was this which fortified the connection between ownership and
management. For it would be most unwise to come in as a 'sleeping
partner', exposing oneself to responsibility for the debts of the firm
without taking part in its management. For one could then be
ruined, as sleeping partners have indeed been ruined, by the mis-
takes the management had made.

If the firm can be made into a company (or corporation) with
limited liability, the worst that can happen to a shareholder, as a
result of his participation, is that his shares become valueless. A creditor can proceed against the company for payment, but he cannot
proceed against shareholders individually. It must of course be
announced to those who trade with the company that it has this
privilege; but this has proved in practice to be no serious obstacle to
trading. It does however remove an obstacle to the admission of outside shareholders, shareholders who do not themselves take part in
the running of the firm. It therefore removes an obstacle to the
growth of the capital invested in the firm.

It was clearly for the purpose of removing this obstacle that limited
liability was invented. In its absence the capital that was invested in
a firm would be restricted by what the partners (both owners and
managers) could themselves put up, and by what they could borrow.
But what they could borrow would itself be limited by the security
they could offer, and that again would depend upon their personal
wealth. A small group of partners might not be able in this way to
offer much security; but if outsiders will take up shares, carrying
limited liability, the total capital invested in the firm can be much increased. A creditor therefore has better security, since he is more
likely to be able to recover *from the firm* even though he loses the
right to recover from shareholders individually.

It is true that even in the absence of limited liability a firm could
grow, by reinvestment of profits; so it could become large, but it
could not start large. The development of such industries as need to

make large investments of capital in order to produce at all would be
severely hampered. Thus it is not surprising that the building of rail-
ways is historically connected with the coming of limited liability.

At this stage, when the purpose is just to enable entrepreneurs to
get control of more capital than they could put up themselves, or
borrow on bonds or debentures, it would seem that the 'ownership'
of the company, by the shareholders who are thus introduced, can be
no more than nominal. The shareholders, by law, have the right to
elect the directors; but the directors are in place before a first issue of
shares is made, and the shareholders show, by subscribing, that they
have no desire to turn those directors out. Thus, whatever be the
legal position, the fact is that capital is being provided by shareholders, just as it would be by bondholders, only on different terms.
While the bondholder is promised a fixed rate of interest, the shareholder is promised a share in profits. The shareholder is much more
like a bondholder than he appears to be in legal theory. That this is
the right way of looking at the matter is shown by the fact that the
terms of an equity issue can be varied, just as security offered to
bondholders can be varied, by adjusting the capital that the proprietors, becoming directors, are supposed to be putting up and indeed
in other ways. That is how the limited liability company begins.

Now how has it been possible to raise capital on these peculiar
terms—capital which, it must be supposed, could not be raised, or
not so advantageously raised, by borrowing at fixed interest? This is
a key question; it will be convenient, when attempting to answer it,
to take it in two stages, beginning with the case in which the shares
are not freely transferable, and going on to the more important case
when they are. Only in the latter, of course, can there be a market in
the shares. But the former is quite a real case. It extends beyond the
case of the private company, or non-quoted company, where there
are legal constraints on transferability; for there may be *de facto* restrictions, as when the new shareholders are no more than a moderate extension of the small group who have direct knowledge of the
business, to people who have personal knowledge of the directors, or
some personal relation with them. It will be useful to begin with this
private company case, since it brings out by contrast how important
is transferability.

Already in the case of non-transferable shares, we have to consider
the matter from two points of view: that of the investor who is to buy
the shares, and that of the company, as represented by the director,

which is to issue them. Take first the investor's position. Why should he buy shares, when he could have invested in bonds? That the equity investment may be regarded as a hedge against inflation is an argument in its favour which in some recent years may have been of importance; but it may here be disregarded, for at the time when limited liability first prospered, it cannot have been significant. There must have been another advantage which was the attraction.

One may look at the matter in terms of the probabilities of return[1] which are offered on the two alternatives. All that has to be considered, when the share is to be non-transferable, is the annual return which is to be expected in some representative future year. If the capital had been raised on the bond, it could only have been so raised if there were a strong probability that the interest agreed would be paid; there would nevertheless be a (usually small) probability that the borrower would be unable to pay, so that a part, or the whole, of what had been invested would be lost. In the case of the share, it is useful to suppose that there is some *most probable return*, which plays much the same part as the agreed return on the bond. The maximum that can be lost, when there is limited liability, is the same as with the bond—total loss of all that has been invested. The probability of total loss is however greater, since the claims of bondholders must be met before there is anything to distribute on the shares. The probability of partial loss—a return which is significantly less than that which appeared to be the most probable—is clearly much greater in the case of the share. Both of these are disincentives to investing in shares. What is there to be set against them? It might seem at first sight that all that there is to set against them is the possibility of a return which is greater than the most probable return; this is zero in the case of the bond, but in the case of the share can be substantial. One of the attractions of shareholding, as against bondholding, may be the possibility of what one might call extra gains.

But it is unlikely that it is the only attraction. If it were to be the main attraction, the investor would have to be a bit of a gambler—who may be defined as a person who is willing to swap a high probability of a moderate loss against a low probability of a gain that is large in comparison. It is not to be denied that a propensity to gamble is one of the things which explains the growth of equity investment.

[1] Probability in the non-technical sense as might be used in business transactions. There is no scope in this discussion for the concepts of mathematical probability theory (see Appendix).

But the extra gains that are possible from investing in a share with restricted transferability can rarely be large enough to arouse the propensity to gamble. There must be something else.

What that is emerges as soon as we consider the alternatives from the company's point of view. When saying that the agreed return on the bond and the most probable return on the share were comparable, it was not implied that they would be equal. There is a good reason why the return on the share should be higher. It is in the interest of the company—as represented here by the former proprietors—to offer a prospect of a higher return on the share, because (so long as the question of control does not arise) finance by share issue diminishes risk.

Interest would have to be paid in good and bad times alike; but in bad times the dividends could be reduced, so the burden of finance by shares would be less. It is true that it would be expected that in good times the dividend would be increased; but it is just in such times that an increased out-payment can most easily be borne. The firm would be insuring itself, against a strain which in difficult times could be serious, at the cost of an increased payment in conditions when it would be easy to meet it. It is in this sense that the riskiness of its position would be diminished.

Thus it would be worth its while to offer a premium, in terms of most probable dividend, to offset the other disadvantages, to the investor, of investing in shares, which of course would remain.[2]

All this applies to the private company, where the circle of shareholders is restricted, and (usually in consequence) the funds that can be raised from them are restricted. Much more can be done if transferability is permitted. The positions of all parties are then transformed.

There can in the first place be a much stronger appeal to the propensity to gamble. When transferability is restricted, the investor must expect to wait quite a time for the possibility of extra gains; and

---

[2] I think this analysis does get to the root of the matter; but we may also have to distinguish between the probabilities, as they appear to the 'insiders' who are raising the capital and as they appear to 'outside' investors. The 'insiders' may be expected to have better information on which to base their estimate. A major objective of company law has been to diminish this inequality of information. If that endeavour has some success—it can never be wholly successful—it diminishes the risks to the investor of investing in shares. And that should be favourable to growth of equity investment, for if the risk to the investor is diminished, it should be easier to persuade him to 'bite'.

when they appear (if they do appear) they can hardly be 'glittering prizes'. But when the share is transferable, there is a chance that it will be possible to sell it at a profit, even in the quite short run. I put this first because in the case of a new issue, it is the motive which comes in first. Big issues of shares are most easily placed when there is a bull market, when the market most closely resembles what Keynes called it, a 'casino'.[3] And the association of share issue with a bull market is one that goes both ways.

This is because the transferable share, carrying limited liability, is a liquid asset. It is not as liquid as cash, or as the closer substitutes for cash; but it is liquid in the looser sense that it can be turned into cash, at short notice, whenever cash is required. So the successful speculator can take his profit, whenever it seems good to him to take it. Even if he does not sell, he has a security against which he can borrow, then perhaps using the proceeds of the loan to buy more shares. Thus a speculative boom is built up. Where does the money come from to support it? The answer, as economists now are well aware (though it took them much trouble to find it), is that the market as a whole, meaning by that the total of all those who are dealing on the market, because it is regarding the share as a liquid asset, is willing to hold less of its assets in monetary form than it was before the boom started. New shares, the dazzling prospects of which have been well advertised, are ideal as a speculative counter.

But though it is in the bull market that shares are most easily placed (and therefore from the point of view of the issuing firm most cheaply placed) they will have in the end to be held; and at that stage those who hold them must surely have a normal risk-aversion. Even so there are advantages, to the investor, of transferability. One of them, still, is the liquidity advantage. The share can still be disposed of, at a price, if the shareholder changes his mind about the prospects of the company or if he wants cash for any other reason. Another, which comes from the combination of limited liability with transfer-

---

[3] I myself rather think that the resemblance to a casino can be overdone. It is well known that the player at Monte Carlo is bound 'in the end' to be a loser, but hopes, irrationally, that this time he will win. (Or perhaps, a little more rationally, that he himself will have the strength of mind to retire from the game at a good moment.) An amateur stock exchange speculator may indeed behave like that, but a boom could get built up entirely by professionals. Their conduct would not be irrational; it would be based on information, but this could be very restricted information, information that was available quickly. Perhaps no more than what the person at the next desk was doing.

ability, but which is not fully effective until the market in shares is well developed, is that the investor can reduce his risks by diversifying his portfolio. Under limited liability, as was shown, the shareholder is made more like a bondholder, in that he cannot lose more than he has put in; so he can imitate the age-old practice of lenders at fixed interest, diminishing his risks by spreading them. It is only the risk of loss on his portfolio as a whole which matters to him. If the securities in which he invests are different, being subject, at least to some extent, to different risks, the risk of loss over the portfolio as a whole is likely to be proportionally less than on any single investment. Without limited liability this could not be done, since investment even in a second enterprise would increase the investor's risks, but with limited liability it can be. It is this, combined with the liquidity advantage, which explains why it is possible to issue shares at no more than a modest 'premium', even though investors are risk-averters.

That is how it happens; but consider the consequences. It is inherent in these advantages, both the liquidity advantage and the practice of risk-spreading, that the individual shareholder, in a fully developed limited liability system, must tend to lose contact, other than a purely financial contact, with the companies of which he is legally part-owner. His right to elect directors must then tend to become a mere formality. There is a way in which this may not happen; but I begin by considering the common case when it does.

The firm is now (we will take it) well established; it has been well established for some considerable time. Who controls it? And on what principles should we expect them to control it?

The first of these questions takes time to come up, for (as we have seen) the original directors are in place at the beginning. But the time will come when they have to be replaced; successors, on occasion, will have to be found. When provision for the election of directors by shareholders has become ineffective, the directors themselves must make provision for succession. It is however by no means evident that the method of providing successors by co-option is any less efficient than that which has to be used in the private business, or partnership. It should indeed be more effective, since in the latter case the choice is likely to be confined to members of a few families, while the directors of a company are not so confined. The company is ruled by what in political terms would be called an oligarchy; but experience seems to show that 'open' oligarchies, which recruit themselves from wider circles, are more efficient and more durable than those where the field for recruitment is narrower.[4]

One may approach the other question by thinking of that which is familiar in examination papers in economics; what does the entrepreneur maximize? So long as one can think of a single entrepreneur in command of a business that belongs to him, there is no doubt what he should be expected to maximize. It is the discounted value of expected net returns—discounted at his individual rate of time-preference. Allowance will have to be made for uncertainty, and perhaps for the toil and trouble involved; but all that is well understood. In the original formation of the limited liability company the same principle, as we have been seeing, will apply. The entrepreneur, at this stage, is the former proprietor, or proprietors, becoming directors; it is the prospective net return, accruing to them, which they will naturally seek to maximize. But after formation it is surely the prospective net return to the shareholders as a whole which they should seek to maximize. That is the legal theory; but when one has gone to our late stage, with a new generation of directors, and shareholders who have lost touch with the company, can that legal theory be realistic? One can more easily see the directors thinking it to be their duty to do their best, not for the shareholders, but for the company. But what, in this sense, is the company?

Before the appearance of transferable shares there would have been no doubt about this; it would have been the proprietors. Afterwards we can get a hint from what was said at the beginning of this chapter about the labour market, about the structure of the firm in terms of the labour which it employs. Here also, on the side of capital structure, a distinction between *nucleus* and *fringe* appears to be required. In the case of the private company, where shareholders are closely attached, there will be no question that on the side of capital they constitute a nucleus. Capital that is borrowed from outside lenders (most definitely when it is expected that the loan will be repaid) will be fringe. In the case of the public company, with shares that are easily transferable, there is no distinction that can be put

---

[4] Corresponding experience in the political field is instructive. Was there any European monarchy, in the days when kings really ruled, which did not suffer disasters from adhering to the rule of hereditary succession? The papacy, where in effect successors are chosen from a wider circle (for though the college of cardinals is restricted in number, they themselves can be chosen much more widely), has over many centuries done much better. It is interesting that the Russian communists appear to be following the papal example.

into so objective a form. There must however usually be a practical distinction between 'inside' shareholders, who feel themselves to be closely associated with the company, so that (like established labour) they expect to go on holding for considerable periods, and the fleeting population of shareholders who are more loosely attached. All shareholders alike will have to be paid the dividend, but while the outsiders are concerned with no more than the current dividend and with the market value of the shares, the insiders are concerned with the future of the company, and so with the dividends they expect, on their own information, to receive at future dates.

This is enough to give rise to some conflict of interest. The outsider may be expected to desire a dividend as large as possible, but it is, at least to some extent, in the interest of the insider that profits should be retained. Why then should it be the practice of companies, which the system leads to be controlled by insiders, to pay anything more than a nominal dividend? The answer seems to be that it is in the interest of the company, even when that is interpreted as we have been coming to interpret it, to keep up the market value of its shares. And this, being formed by outsiders, is likely to be strongly affected by the current dividend.

The traditional reason for desiring a strong value of shares is that it makes it easier for the company to borrow; but this, since large retentions make borrowings less necessary, cuts both ways. A more important reason, in recent times, but not only in recent times, concerns take-overs and mergers.

A take-over bid, in the light of what has been said, may be regarded as a counter-attack by shareholders who, in the course of the process described, have been so nearly pushed out. Although a 'change of government' as a result of a discussion at an annual meeting is not practicable, the market has provided an alternative. The prices at which a company's shares are normally valued are based on the expectation that the company will continue under the same management; for the sale of a few shares by one individual and their purchase by another is unlikely to affect any voting. If however a company's policy is such that an outsider can feel sure that it is not doing its best for its shareholders, it will be worth his while to offer higher prices for large blocks of shares, in order to acquire enough voting power to change the management, either in person or in policy. Having brought about this revolution, the shares can again be sold; and if the prospects of the company, as assessed by the market, then seem to be sufficiently improved, they can be sold at a profit. When directors have got themselves into the habit of mind (the origins of which have been explained) of thinking that they are working for the interest of the 'company', or even of the 'public', or for anything other than the interests of their shareholders, they may, in accordance with the legal position, lay themselves open to a flank attack on these lines.

The outsider who makes the bid will itself in most cases be a company; and it will be easier for it to make the bid if its own shares are strong. For on the one hand it will then be possible to offer shareholders in the weak company shares in the strong company in exchange; and on the other, if cash has to be offered, the cash can more easily be borrowed. Thus it is not only weak companies which have an interest to see that the value of their shares is maintained, for defensive reasons; it is also strong companies who have a corresponding incentive, so as to make it easier for them to expand by acquisitions. When the two incentives are taken together, they cover a good part of the ground; so the position of the shareholder is stronger than might appear at first sight.

The take-over sanction has on the whole a good reputation among economists; but we should distinguish. There is no doubt that in the case of a management that has gone sleepy, or has forgotten to keep its eye on profitability, it has an economic function; the quality of management should be improved. But this is by no means the only thing that can happen. Take the case, at the other extreme, of two firms which are competing in the sale of their products. The stronger may buy up the weaker just to get rid of a competitor. It can be a cheaper way of doing this than by 'cut-throat competition', forcing it into bankruptcy. So the availability of the take-over may in the end facilitate monopolistic practices, thus protecting inefficiencies which it might have been expected to obviate.

Yet there is more to be said for an alternative which may be hard to distinguish from this last. If the firm taken over is absorbed into a 'group', that also may be conducive to monopolistic behaviour but need not be. This will happen if the members are left with powers of initiative, the 'centre' retaining little more than some functions which are clearly appropriate to it. Two of these have emerged from what has here been said. One is providing help over succession of managers; the other is financial. The 'centre' naturally acts as a bank for the group—a bank which, because of its closer and probably more permanent association, can keep in closer touch with the needs of members than an outside bank could do.

We saw in Chapter 7 that it is to an arrangement of this sort that a banking system itself is likely to tend. There is no reason why it should not show its strength also outside the banking field. The ultimate reason for it is that the conventional unit of production is subject in different ways to scale economies; the 'optimum' in one direction may be different from that in another. It makes for efficiency to separate them out; when that can be done consistently with co-operation.

PART III

PROBLEMS AND POLICIES

11 The Old Trade Cycle

That the work of Keynes was a turning-point, between one epoch of economic thinking and another, has been shown in several ways in previous chapters of this book. That it was associated with another turning-point, in what economists call the 'real world', has not been given the same attention. He was writing during and just after the world economic crisis of 1929–34; this is background to what he is saying. At that time it was obvious to his readers that there was this association; not only his occasional pieces, to be collected as *Essays in Persuasion*, but also his major works, had a topical side to them. They reflected his perception of what was going on around him—the passage from one way of organizing economic affairs to what would have to be another.

Other economists—I think one may safely say, most other economists then engaged in writing and teaching—did not see it like that. They had their own idea of what was happening; they looked upon it as an example, admittedly a major example, of a familiar type of disturbance which was called the trade cycle or business cycle. It was already many years since that had first been recognized. We may perhaps date the beginning of its recognition (in Britain at least) to the work of Jevons in the 1870s. This is important, not in itself (for his sunspot theory of cycles did not stand up to investigation) but because of the belief, on which it was founded, that something was happening which was sufficiently repetitive to warrant analysis by some sort of scientific method. There could be no doubt after Jevons that a question at least had been asked.

We need however to understand that the cycles, which Jevons and his immediate successors had in mind, were not the statistical cycles so well known to the modern economist. These can be found in any time-series, of any variable, not at all necessarily economic. The current observation is greater or less than its predecessor; the series is going up or going down. A single rise or fall, we admit, is not significant; but the statisticians have been busy in giving us tests of significance, which largely consist in the fitting of the observations into a cyclical pattern. Mere continuance of the motion in the same direction gives a crude test of significance; as when the market analysts say that a fall in an index, continuing for three quarters, may be called a recession. But we do not want a rise that starts from a low point, and never gets far from that low point, to have the same significance as one that starts high. What however is 'high' or 'low'? It must be with reference to some norm, or standard. One can construct a norm by purely statistical methods, fitting a trend, and judging the actuals by reference to the trend. Most economic series do not jump about very much from one observation to the next (for the observations are snapshots of what in fact is a continuing process); so when there is a deviation from trend which is at all considerable it will usually last for a number of observations. There will be sequences of pluses and sequences of minuses; and it is easy for these to begin to look like a cycle.

I want to insist that this is *not* what Jevons and his contemporaries can have had in mind; for the statistical apparatus of trend-fitting had not in their time come into use. They were thinking of the sequence of trade *crises* which had marked the preceding half-century, occurring in 1825, 1837 (possibly[1]), 1847, 1857, and 1867; that looked very much like a ten-year cycle (which would match the sunspots!). These crises were striking events; even the earlier ones had received a good deal of attention from economists,[2] though it

[1] For it was more important in the US than in Europe.

[2] And others. Thomas Love Peacock, whose satirical novels are still worth reading, wrote a piece entitled 'Pan in town' on the 1825 crisis. (Pan is the god of pan-ic.) I cannot resist quoting a few lines of it.

Pan:　The country banks are breaking
　　The London banks are shaking
　　Suspicion is awaking
　　E'en quakers now are quaking:
　　Experience seems to settle
　　That paper is not metal,
　　And promises of payment
　　Are neither food nor raiment . . .
Chorus:　Our balances, our balances
　　Our balances, our balances
　　Pay—pay—pay—pay
　　Without delay
　　Our balances, our balances.
(Enter Scottish economist)
Economist:　A weel sirs, what's the matter?
　　An' hegh sirs, what's the clatter?
　　　Ye dinna ken
　　　Ye seely men,
　　Your fortunes ne'er were better.

was not until the time of Jevons that the series as listed was complete. So it was not until then that the periodicity could be recognized (of course it is clear from later experiences that too much attention was given to it, not only by Jevons). Nevertheless, though the periodicity may have been dubious, there was not much doubt about the repetition.

Not enough attention has later been paid to the useful discussion of the earlier crises which is to be found in the *Principles* of John Stuart Mill (1848), surely the standard work on principles of economics belonging to that central Victorian period. Mill did not have the whole story before him; but what he says about the part on which he did have information is good. The cycle was a financial cycle. There was a boom, with rising prices and then rising interest rates; it led to a crisis, with a wave of bankruptcies. The unemployment which followed was a consequence of the bankruptcies, or of attempts to avoid them. After the crisis prices fell; rates of interest then came down. The latter was a first step on the road to recovery.

Mill was already able to show how this could happen.[3] A general rise in prices—many prices rising, few falling—would require to be financed. It could at first be financed by trade credit (as described in Chapters 5 and 6 in this book). The buyer got the goods at the expense of an increase in his debts. But trade credit though expansible would not be indefinitely expansible; the time would come when some of the extended trade had to be financed by something commanding wider confidence. Recourse would then be had to the banking system, and there would be an expansion of bank money. But even bank money (then) might not be thought of as being reliable enough; so there would come to be an increased demand for the really solid money, the gold coins which were then in common circulation. The custodian of the central gold reserve was the Bank of England; it had a reserve but it was very limited. So when the Bank was in sight of the point at which it would be unable to exchange its notes for gold, it had to take action to enforce a restriction on

There's too much population
And too much cultivation
That's a' that ails the nation.

So he sends them off to a lecture on the principles of banking. But the bank has nothing but Chilean bonds to pay them with.

[3] *Principles*, Book III, Chapter 12. His essay 'On the influence of consumption on production' in *Essays on Unsettled Questions* (1844) needs to be read with it.

borrowing. That was the crisis. The rising interest rates which preceded the crisis showed that some people saw it approaching.

In the crisis, weak positions were uncovered, and there were
failures. But the Bank itself survived, and most of the banks survived.
The pressure then relaxed; interest rates, being symptoms of the pressure, came down. When the debris had been cleared up, so that
nearly all firms which survived were of unquestioned solvency, an
'equilibrium', as it might be called, would be restored. But it would be
an unstable equilibrium, since it was just from such that the former
boom had started. Sooner or later the cycle would be re-enacted.

There are two particular characteristics of this classical (or
Jevonian) cycle which need to be emphasized. One is that at the time
in question Britain, beyond doubt, was the economic centre of the
world. So it is perfectly proper, for that time, to treat the British experience, as *the* experience; much of what happened in other countries just followed from it. The other is that in this period the Gold
Standard was sacred; in Britain it was sacred. There was no question
(it was known that there was no question) that the convertibility of
Bank of England notes, and deposits, into gold at a fixed parity must
be maintained. It was this which in the end provided a firm ceiling on
expansion, a monetary ceiling. It was known that the expansion
could not go on indefinitely; so, as the boom developed, people began
to take precautions. Wise men had battened down the hatches before
the storm broke.

There was also the question, known to be the more difficult question, of providing a floor. Prices, particularly of primary commodities,
would fall at the crisis; but if the cycle was to continue (or if there
was to be a return to equilibrium) they must be stopped from going
on falling. How should that be? They had fallen in the crisis, not
because they had been thought to be 'too high', but because the
money that was needed to support them had been lacking; bear
speculation, selling to buy back later, would nevertheless have been
a feature of the fall. One can see that a point would be reached (there
is plenty of experience of its being reached) when the balance of
opinion among speculators would turn in favour of the fall having
gone too far, so they would begin to speculate for a rise, at first very
tentatively. Such speculation is stabilizing; it needs to be encouraged.

It does not appear that Mill had got so far as to see this, though it is
stated in a much earlier work of which he made use—the *Paper
Credit* of Henry Thornton (1802). There it appears in a context

which by the middle of the century had become very historical; so the whole of its relevance to current concerns may not have been obvious, even to Mill. The *Thornton precept* (as I shall call it, for he deserves to have his name attached to it) was in two parts. The first necessity, when the crisis has arisen, is for the centre of the system (in his case, or Mill's, the Bank of England) to ensure its own security; for that purpose it must maintain high rates of interest, so as to draw funds to itself, to replenish its reserves. However, when that has been done, it should turn over decisively to the other tack, with the aim of spreading security from itself to the rest of the banking system, and then outside. The two belong together.[4]

The Thornton precept does not only mean, and perhaps does not even principally mean, that rates of interest which have risen in the crisis, and indeed on the way to the crisis, should come down as soon as it is safe for the Bank to reduce them. For it should not be taken for granted that offers to lend, at low rates of interest, to *suitable borrowers*, will in such conditions be easily taken up. Active lending presupposes confidence, on the part both of the lender and of the borrower; *and* of the borrower, because of the lender in the borrower, for how should the (now) selective lender have confidence in the borrower if the borrower cannot give reason for feeling that confidence himself? That loans are available at low rates, from one part of the central nucleus of the banking system to another—between well-established banks, or from them to other well-established financiers—does not necessarily imply that they are so easily available outside. The essential point of the Thornton precept is that after a crisis, when that has been a considerable crisis, the financial system, and the rest

---

[4] The name which later writers have commonly associated with what I call the Thornton precept is that of Walter Bagehot (*Lombard Street*, 1873). Bagehot does say explicitly, on his page 209: 'The best palliative to a panic is a confidence in the adequate amount of the bank reserve, and in the efficient use of that reserve.' This no doubt was meant to mean much the same thing as was meant by Thornton. It may just be that because the banking system with which Thornton is concerned is simpler, the principles on which he is basing the precept seem to me to come out more clearly than they do in Bagehot. It was not until 1939, on the publication of a reprint of *Paper Credit*, that Dennis Robertson, who needed it, read the Thornton book. But I remember what he said to me years later, when I told him that I was giving a lecture on Thornton, to be reprinted in my *Critical Essays*: 'Oh, Thornton, he knew everything.' He did indeed have all the essentials of the theory of monetary policy, of which Robertson had made himself the champion. He was nearer to Robertson than he was to Hayek, who wrote the introduction to the reprint. I doubt if Keynes ever had an opportunity to study Thornton, or indeed on these matters, even Mill. The 'classics' he did study were less help to him than they would have been.

of the economy, so far as that is dependent on the financial system, needs to be nursed back to health.

If this had been accepted—and it may be that by the 1870s it was by the more far-seeing bankers beginning to be accepted—it could be maintained that though the financial system had no sure means of maintaining an 'equilibrium', it did have means of correcting excessive departure from it. There was no doubt that it was possible for leading banks by acting together to prevent 'overheating'; and if the *precept* were followed they would have at least some means of combating a divergence in the other direction. Violent swings, as experience showed, were damaging; but if the remedial measures were promptly and adequately taken, the swings would be damped and so made less harmful. That however implied that there was someone, or some body, that was in a position to take the action required. In that crucial sense the system needed to have a *centre*.

It would not necessarily be implied that this should be what we now think of as a Central Bank. A Central Bank, we have in later days come to take for granted, is a bank which—whether or not it is actually set up by government—has a close relation to government; it is a part of what in a wide sense may be called the political structure of the country in which it is operating. But a centre need not begin in that way. As we saw in the previous chapter on banking (Chapter 7), because of the risks to which any bank is in principle subject, a banking system as such has a tendency to develop a centre, being a bank, or group of banks, on which other banks come to rely. This can come about without any action by government. The relation so established can indeed transcend the boundaries of nations. It is not inevitable that the centre and the circle of banks dependent upon it should be situated in the same country. This was already apparent in the British case in what we may call the post-Jevonian period. London was acting as a centre, not only for the British banking system in a narrow sense, but also for banks in the then far-flung British Empire, and even for banks in countries which were in no political sense British, some South American countries being at that time leading examples. The circle for which the Bank of England was centre was a very extensive circle. That may well have made it easier for the Bank to pursue a stabilizing policy. We do in fact find that in the days of Marshall and Edgeworth financial crises were mild; the financial cycle was almost disappearing.

But for this it is likely that there will have been another reason.

Though Britain was retaining much of her financial leadership, the economic leadership which she had possessed in the middle of the century was going. Most of the 1880s were years of depression in England; but they were not years of depression in Germany or in the United States. It is indeed inevitable, when countries are on a common standard (in this case a gold standard) and are committed to the maintenance of that standard, that those which are lagging (as we should now say, in terms of productivity) will not be able to 'let themselves go' in the way the stronger countries can do. So the booms which they can allow themselves will have to be weak. Though their 'growth' over the cycle as a whole will be less than that of the others, nevertheless within the cycle they are likely to be more stable.

So I do not need to say more about the British story, in the sequel to the Jevons period. The British had more or less solved their problem; but by the end of the century the scene was shifting to the United States. The US, at the time in question, had no Central Bank; to have one was thought to be inconsistent with their political principles; it was too central an institution to fit a federation. Nevertheless when the need arose a substitute was found, one which at first did not do so badly. The American banking system, as we should expect (see again Chapter 7), was finding a centre for itself; it consisted of the big New York banks, on which the rest had come to depend. In the (American) crisis of 1893 that worked. The New York banks acting together, however informally, were strong enough to carry through a Thornton-type policy.

Nevertheless on the next occasion (1907) when there was a strain, it was a greater strain, and it became doubtful if what had been done on the former occasion was sufficient. Some (at least temporary) more formal arrangement appeared to be required. But these were the days of President 'Teddy' Roosevelt and his war on 'Trusts', industrial combinations, centres of economic power that were thought to be dangerous. Presidential approval of the bankers' arrangement had thus to be sought; and though in the end it was got, it was hard to get it.[5] So, after 1907, it became accepted (1) that some sort of a formal centre was needed and (2) that it must be federal, explicitly federal. This was the origin of the Federal Reserve System (the 'Fed'), legislation for which was passed in 1912, though

[5] I have been helped by the lively account of this in the essay on Pierpont Morgan in J. R. T. Hughes, *The Vital Few*.

it did not begin to operate until November 1914, after the beginning of war in Europe. Thus for no fault of its own, it had a difficult start. Its behaviour between 1914 and 1921 has been much criticized, but it is hard to see that the criticisms go very deep. War-time inflation could hardly have been avoided by any policy; and, what may be the most important test, recovery from the slump of 1921 was remarkably quick.

The events of 1929–33 were very different. We now know that the policy of the 'Fed' at that time had much to do with the disaster which occurred. It has been shown[6] that in its early years it had been much under the influence of experienced New York bankers, personified by the New York governor, Benjamin Strong; but he died in 1928. Thereafter policy was determined by a majority of governors of 'member banks', many of them coming from the fringes of the banking system. They had not learned how to act as *central* bankers. They did not realize that the reserves, that could be available to the 'Fed', were immensely strong; they did not need a great deal of fortification. They were thinking of their own regional banks, which did need fortifying, but could have been fortified from the centre. So as this was neglected, they went on clinging to the first part of the Thornton precept, and forgot the second.

The result was just what a Thorntonian could have predicted. About a year after the Wall Street crash, when (if his policy had been followed) there should have been signs of recovery, there was a secondary crisis, still largely confined to the US, when many banks, and not only banks, closed their doors. But the pressure was kept up, and in 1931 it happened again. This time Europe also was involved. Leading European countries at that date had returned (after the War) to a gold standard, but a very fragile gold standard, largely supported by American credit. So we may think of the 'Fed' as having a circle of banks dependent upon it, not only within but also outside America. Foreigners could however protect themselves, in the emergency, by abandoning their fixed link with the dollar, 'going off gold'.[7] This is what they did, a good many of them did, beginning with the floating of the British pound in September 1931.

[6] I have been deeply influenced, in this interpretation, by what I have leaned from the massive researches of Friedman and Schwartz, *Monetary History of the United States* (1963). What happened in 1929–33 has been made much clearer by them than it was before. The monetarist form in which their analysis is put has little effect on the substance of their argument.

[7] I cannot resist inserting a personal recollection. In those years I was a junior lecturer at LSE. I had been working on labour problems; I knew very little about money.

From the point of view of a country which took this course, it was in itself a release. For the position of its Central Bank, *in terms of its own currency*, was now secure; it was free, as soon as it was clear that internal confidence in the currency had not been damaged, to take remedial action. So it was that already in the summer of 1932, rates of interest in London began to come down. It took time for this to exercise much effect on activity, but it was a first step on the road to recovery.

It must however be emphasized that the condition laid down, of internal confidence in the currency not being damaged, was essential for this (relatively) favourable outcome. One needs to recognize that for a country such as Germany (still at that time a constitutional republic) the British way out was probably not open. For the Great Inflation, which had destroyed the internal value of the German Mark, was then less than a decade away; confidence in its successor could not be counted on; a flight from it could be easily aroused. So it may well be that the only course which was open was rigorous exchange control—which prepared the way for Hitler.[8]

Whichever way it was that other countries reacted, the effect on the US itself was much the same. The overseas assets of American banks, which they had been encouraged to build up (to help in post-war reconstruction) were suddenly devalued in terms of dollars. So there was another round of American bank failures, continuing through 1932—in America the worst year of the Depression—and culminating in the general closure of banks, as Franklin Roosevelt took office, in March 1933. That was the end of the old 'Fed'. The American Government had to take power to support the banking system, details of which I do not have to discuss. Other countries, in one way or another, followed this example. The old style of financial cycle, which has been the subject of this chapter, thus came to an end.

In July 1931, at the time when the monetary crisis erupted in Germany, I met our monetary expert, Theodore Gregory, who had just been working with Keynes on the Macmillan Committee. I asked him, in my innocence: what does this mean? 'The whole of Europe,' he said, 'will be off the gold standard within a week.' He was very well informed; if he had said two months he would have been about right. That has always been a lesson to me on economists' predictions.

[8] I may support this with another anecdote. In September 1931, Ursula Webb, who was to become my wife, was studying in Vienna. She used to relate how the famous Austrian economist, L. von Mises, proclaimed at his seminar: 'In one week, England will be in a hyper-inflation!' That was ridiculous, applied to England; I used, for many years, to think it was ridiculous. But would it have been so if applied to Austria—or Germany? Recent experience in South America seems to leave this an open question.

12 The Credit Economy: Wicksell

The issue between the two theories of interest, which was discussed in Chapter 9, could, in the light of what has now been said, have been looked at in another way. Each made interest determined at a particular margin, but the choice margins to which they directed attention were different. For Marshall it was a choice between bonds and goods—consumption goods on the savers' side, investment goods on the other. For Keynes it was a choice between holding bonds and holding money, a non-interest-bearing money. Keynesians often insisted that since it was a money rate of interest that was in question, it was the latter margin which must be of decisive importance. If Marshall was to determine a money rate of interest in his manner, he must be assuming that the price-level of (either sort of) goods was fairly stable, or at least that by his 'savers' and 'investors' no persisting change in it, over a relevant future, was contemplated. At the time when he was writing, would that have been such a bad assumption? He would nevertheless have been obliged to admit, if he had lived to face the issue, that it had become a much worse assumption by the time of Keynes. And, in spite of the invention of index-linked bonds, it is not a very appealing assumption now.[1]

Nevertheless, if Marshall was put out of date by Keynes, has not much the same thing happened to Keynes's own theory, at least in the form he gave it in his most famous book? It is just that form of his theory which is affected; the more general theory of choice among assets, as set out in Chapter 8 (deeply influenced by his work) remains. What has happened is that the non-interest-bearing money, on which his argument depended, has changed its character. Of course it still exists; but it has largely lost its function as a reserve

---

[1] If it were the case that all (or most) medium-term lending was index-linked, Marshall might come back into his own. It would certainly be a *real* rate of interest which would be determined in his manner; is there any other way it could be determined? I suspect that it is a model of this type which is often in the minds of economic commentators; and in their context I am prepared to give it some countenance myself. It is to their world that it seems to belong. I cannot however believe that there are many actual financial transactions which proceed in terms of (even subjective) real rates. If they did, then surely index-linking would have made more impact than it seems to have done.

asset, at the most liquid end of a spectrum of assets, the position which at the time of Keynes it was natural to think of it as occupying. When short rates of interest were as low as they were at that time, there seemed to be continuity between cash, which did not yield interest, and bills (and time-deposits) which did, but so very little. So, as we have seen, it was natural for Keynes and his immediate followers to take them together, neglecting the fact that some deposits did bear interest, treating them all as *money*.

The much higher (short) rates of interest to which, in so many countries, we have become accustomed in the seventies and eighties, have made this no longer possible. It is no longer so nearly a matter of indifference whether liquid reserves are held in cash or in 'shorts'. Any rational operator will get out of holding cash, as a reserve, as completely as he can. The cash that he still goes on holding is now not a reserve asset; it is a running asset, like the *goods in process* in the balance-sheet of a manufacturer. It is dependent on the money values of the business he is doing; but there is not much room for choice about the ratio between them. A gulf has opened between that circulating money and the most liquid of his reserves.

It was tempting, once this had been perceived, to suppose that the way was open to a much simpler system of control than either Keynes or Marshall had contemplated, that to which the name of 'monetarism' has been given. If the circulating money could be identified, and if the *velocity* with which it entered into the purchase of output was independent of economic incentives (so that it could be taken to be fairly constant), control of the quantity of that circulating money should enable the value of output (Keynes's Y) to be controlled. But how should this quantity be controlled? There would be no direct way that was open to the banking system for controlling it. All it could do would be to adjust its lending policy, changing the rate, or rates, of interest that it was charging to borrowers (possibly also changing a system of 'credit rationing' that it was practising), watching the quite roundabout effects of these on Y, then accepting the effects of these on circulating money. Monetarism gets cause and effect the wrong way round. So it offers no short-cut.

At modern rates of interest, to hold barren money even as a running asset has become costly; so it must be expected that means for economizing in it will be looked for and will be found—as surely they have! We are on the way to a credit economy, in which any money that does not bear interest has become no more than small change, or petty cash. It is surely as least as tolerable a simplification as others to which an economic theorist is accustomed to take it that this has already happened. That is what I shall do in the rest of this chapter.

Money remains of course a standard of value, in terms of which people do their calculations, and in terms of which debts are expressed. But money as means of payment is just a debt. The payment of a debt is an exchange of debts. We regard it as payment because the debts have different quality. It is quality from the point of view of the creditor that matters. I pay my creditor with a cheque on a bank; he accepts it, because he has more confidence in a debt from the bank than he has in a debt from me. Even if he kept his own account at a different bank from mine, he will usually accept it as a money payment; debts from the one bank and from the other have, from the points of view of all concerned, equal reliability. If however I had drawn my cheque on a bank of which he had never heard, and which (so far as he could tell) might be purely imaginary, he would not have accepted it as a payment.

One can construct, in the light of this consideration, two pure models of a credit economy, each of which has its uses. I call them the *monocentric* and *polycentric* respectively.

It is characteristic of a monocentric model that it has just one *central* entity, promises to pay by which have superior quality, or reputation, than those of any other entity. The continuance of that superiority is taken for granted, so that there is just this one 'monetary authority'. The polycentric model has no such single centre. But there will still be differences in the qualities of promises by different entities; so there will be some, at any particular moment, which have highest quality. If there is one which at the moment has the highest quality, it acts, for the moment, like a monocentre; but there is no certainty that it will retain that position. It may be, on the other hand, that there are several that have established an equal reliability, each maintaining a willingness to convert its promises, at a fixed rate, into those of the others. If there is perfect convertibility, each has some of the properties of a monocentre, but there is no single 'monetary authority'.

It will surely be noticed that a monocentric model is likely to have most relevance to the problems of a national economy, especially when the international aspects of that economy—external trade and capital movements—are being left out of account. The polycentric model has most relevance to international problems. I shall have enough to do in the present chapter if I confine myself to the former. The latter is postponed to Chapter 14, since it needs more preparation.

The simplest example of a monocentric model is that constructed, not long after the time that Marshall was writing, by Knut Wicksell.[2] There is just one bank, providing credit money, the only money there is, and there are no other financial bodies. The only form in which savings can be held is as deposits in the bank, and it is only from the bank that those undertaking investment can borrow. The only means of control that is available to the bank is the rate of interest it pays (and charges). This is the basic *money rate* of interest.

It is tempting to say that a system such as this would be *in equilibrium* over a period, if the net increase in the volume of loans being made by the bank was equal to the net increase in the volume of savings deposits. For this would mean that the volume of money that was circulating outside the bank would be remaining unchanged over the period. Wicksell himself was sometimes inclined to this 'monetarist' interpretation of equilibrium, but the model is by no means committed to it. There is another criterion, which also makes its appearance in Wicksell's work, according to which the system is in equilibrium if the price-level is remaining constant. The equilibrium rate of interest is then that which maintains constant prices. But there is more in that direction that can be said.

There are after all many indices of prices, which do not always move together; so there should be an equilibrium rate of interest corresponding to each. One of them is a wage index, so there should be an equilibrium rate which would keep the wage-level constant. Or if wages are *sticky*, it could be interpreted as that which would give a desired level of employment (in the manner of Keynes). And if it is not the wage-level which has become sticky, but a conventional rate of rise in the wage-level which has become sticky, there could be an equilibrium rate of interest which (in the same sense) would fit that rate of rise in the wage-level. To keep the money rate of interest at that level would not cure inflation; all it could do would be to ensure, by being high enough, that monetary policy was not in itself aggravating the inflation; and, by being low enough, that the activity of the

---

[2] *Geldzins und Güterpreise* (1898); the English translation, *Interest and Prices*, was not available until 1939. Its influence on English economics goes further back, for in the thirties there were some of us who did read German!

economy was not being depressed by monetary policy. All these things are in sight of what I may call the original Wicksell model.

But this is not the only direction in which it needs to be developed. For what about uncertainty, and costs of making transactions, which I have repeatedly emphasized to be at the heart of monetary theory? Let us try to put them back and see what happens.

Not much needs to happen on the side of the savers. Their deposits in the bank are certain; they can deposit what they like and will get the rate of interest which the bank is offering, to all alike. But on the side of the bank's advances it is a different story. We must no longer think of the bank just fixing a rate of interest at which it is willing to lend, letting anyone who is prepared to pay that rate have the money. The bank will have to attend to the prospects of particular borrowers and to their character; so whether, in its judgement, they can be relied on to repay. This is a question of the information which is available to the bank.

One can conceive of a situation when the bank was receiving deposits but was finding it difficult to find suitable borrowers. It would thus be withdrawing money from circulation; this could go on to such an extent that in none of the senses that have been distinguished could there be an equilibrium. Should one then say that the money rate is too high? That would only make sense if a way out could be found by lowering it. But to lower the rate which the bank was charging to borrowers would not automatically help it to find new trustworthy borrowers; it does not itself provide an automatic way of finding them. (How far it provides a sufficient incentive for existing borrowers to borrow more is a matter I shall be considering in the chapter that follows.) To lower the rate it pays on deposits may do something to discourage deposits; but since savings deposits will for the most part be held as reserves, even a zero rate on deposits may fail to choke them off to the extent which is required.

We are thus already in sight of the famous crux—an excess of 'saving' over 'investment' that by interest policy cannot be righted. But it is too soon to look for a *Deus ex machina*. We should first consider whether we have not been placing too great a responsibility upon our myopic bank.

To insist, as in this First Revision of the Wicksell model we have been doing, that all borrowing and lending must take place through the bank, is quite unnecessary. If the bank is unable to find suitable borrowers, why should not some of the savers search them out for themselves? There is no reason why we should deny them the possibility of making more direct contacts. In so far as they do this, they will have less to deposit with the bank; so the surplus of funds, which we have been supposing to be going into the bank, will be moderated. It should however be noticed that since the alternative of depositing with the bank remains open to the savers, and the liquidity of their lendings to the firms (as it will now be convenient to call them) must be less than that of their deposits in the bank, the rate of interest which is offered by the firms[3] must be greater than the deposit rate of the bank. This will act as a minimum to the system of interest rates which in this Second Revision begins to develop.

It is indeed this deposit rate which acts as the king-pin of the system, playing much the same part as was played by *the* money rate in the original Wicksell model. For the alternative of depositing, at the fixed deposit rate of the bank, is always open to the savers, while the alternative of borrowing directly from the bank is not so regularly open to the firms. We need not exclude the possibility of the bank doing some direct lending to the firms—at a rate which (we should now say) must be somewhat higher than the rate which it was paying on deposits. For the model is now to allow for transaction costs; the bank will have costs of administration and these must be covered. The firms will get what they can at this rate, which we may fairly suppose will be lower than what they pay on direct loans from the savers; but they want more than this, and it can be got from the savers.

It will be noticed that in this Second Revision the bank is less 'central' than it was in the First. But it still retains some power of control, through its deposit rate.

The solution that has so far been found for the information problem is very imperfect; it has really added nothing more than an opportunity for the firms to raise some part of the funds they require by borrowing from their friends. A modern economy does not rely much on that, though there have been times in history when it has been important. Its place has largely been taken by an alternative of much greater potency—the introduction of financial intermediaries, which make a direct attack on the information problem.

---

[3] Or its equivalent, in terms of prospect offered, if the direct lending to the firms takes the form of subscription to equities.

The financial intermediary can prosper[4] if it can make use of specialized knowledge about the prospects of particular kinds of real investment, so that it can make advances to firms, or investments in the securities of firms, which the bank would not know were sound investments; and if it can acquire resources which enable it to make those financial investments at less loss of liquidity than they would entail upon the private saver. But it cannot prosper unless it makes a profit; this implies that it must borrow at a lower rate than that at which it lends, there being a sufficient difference to cover its administrative costs, and to compensate it for the additional risk with which it, in its turn, is involved in every extension of its operations.

Thus its *in-rate* (as we may call it—the rate at which it borrows) and also its *out-rate* will have to be fitted into the structure of rates, which had already appeared in our Second Revision. It is not necessary that the in-rate of the financial intermediary should be higher than the rate which is paid by the firms (directly) to the bank, or by the firms (directly) to the savers. For it may be expected that the intermediary may be able to attract funds from the bank and from the savers, by offering a greater degree of security (by pooling of risks) than the firms could do directly. And it need not necessarily charge a lower out-rate than is charged by the bank, since it will be willing to do business with the firms which the bank would not do. It is however clear that its in-rate must be appreciably higher than the bank's deposit rate, and its out-rate must be higher than its in-rate, if it is to function at all.

It will surely be granted that this Third Revision has brought our post-Wicksell model quite a step nearer reality. The particular institutions which play the parts I have assigned to 'bank' and 'intermediaries' (even to 'firms' and 'savers') will no doubt differ from country to country, and from one time to another. But that some will be found who play something like the parts in question can hardly be doubted, though it may take some thought to find them.

For instance, I accept that the *bank*, as it appears in a Wicksell or post-Wicksell model, differs from a Central Bank, as that appears in practice, in a way which would appear to be essential. We would not expect a Central Bank to accept deposits from all and sundry; so it does not have a deposit rate which it can use as a means of control. If

---

[4] I here borrow a passage which first appeared in my *Capital and Growth* (1965, pp. 266–7) and was also used in the paper 'The credit economy', written for the second volume of my *Collected Essays*, on which the whole of this chapter is based.

it accepts deposits (or what amount to deposits) it is only from a limited circle that it is willing to accept them. (So there are intermediaries on this side also.) Nevertheless though its power as a borrower is hardly ever exercised, it remains as a sanction which could be brought into play.

It is evident from British experience (which I cannot help having in mind) that *Minimum Lending Rate*, or *Bank Rate* as it used to be called, does not have to be 'effective'; actual market rates, for loans on similar conditions, would often be below it. In order to make it effective, if it desired to do so, the Bank would have to find some means of withdrawing funds from the market—that is to say, in my terminology, of coming in as a borrower.[5] One must suppose that it was taken for granted that some way of doing this would be discoverable. For once that was accepted, a rise in Bank Rate, taken under conditions and in such a manner[6] as to indicate that the Bank 'meant business', would be followed by commercial banks and by others within the 'circle', without it being necessary for the sanction to be actually used. Once there was this understanding, it would be the whole 'centre' of the banking system (consisting not only of what was called the Central Bank but also of what had become its satellites) which would be acting like the single bank of the Wicksell model.

Indeed, as this shows, the model when taken strictly is one of a system in which all transactions are 'at arm's length', all participants acting independently. It is useful to have such a model, not only because there are people—important people!—who think it to be an ideal arrangement, but also because it is a useful basis with which other arrangements can conveniently be compared. It is, I think, shown up when it is used in that manner that it may be far from being an ideal arrangement.

For let us consider further how an arm's length system could work. I will simplify a little (I think it is only a little) by supposing that marginal funds—those needed for a marginal expansion in an investment programme—will always be raised by the firms from the intermediaries, and by the intermediaries from the bank. There is

---

[5] It is not evident that mere abstention from renewal of short-dated lending could be relied on to be sufficient.

[6] The old Bank of England convention, that a half-point rise in bank rate showed no more than that the Bank was just following the market, while a whole-point rise was meant to give a lead, had its uses as a simple signal.

then a straightforward sequence. The savers deposit in the bank at an interest rate r_0, the bank lends to the intermediaries at an interest rate r_1, and intermediaries lend to the firms at r_2. Rate r_1 must exceed r_0 to cover the administrative costs of the bank; r_2 must exceed r_1 not only because of administrative costs, but also to provide a liquidity premium. So r_2 exceeds r_0 by two margins, those of the bank and of the intermediaries.

And having gone so far, we may allow ourselves to go further. Let us suppose that there is a rate R, which will stand for the return which the firms expect to get from marginal investment; this will have to exceed r_2 by another liquidity premium. We could then say that it would be R which, from the point of view of the Wicksell construction, would need to be kept at an equilibrium level, the level which was appropriate to the kind of equilibrium which it was desired to attain.

All this is involved in an arm's length system. It is inherent in it that there should be a gap, depending on liquidity preferences of the various parties and also on administrative costs, between anything that can be directly controlled by an interest policy *of the bank* and the yield on investment (R) which should be the key to equilibrium. If the gap is narrow, and can be relied on to be narrow, interest policy can be quite effective; but if the gap is wide and undependable, there is a formidable obstacle in its way.

We should however remember that the problem is an information problem. In order to make wise decisions on the big issues which may here be in question, many sorts of information need to be gathered; they can hardly be gathered without having many listening points. The financial intermediaries are listening points; the problem is one of transmission, from them to the centre. It is not obvious that an arm's length system, using the 'price-mechanism', must always be the most efficient, or most 'economic', way of doing this job. It is not always the only way that is open for doing it. When the intermediaries are well established, the relations between them and the centre can be much closer. It seems to follow from what has been said that it is desirable that they should be closer. Control must have power if it is to be effective. Whatever we think about monopoly and competition, in the rest of the economic system, there are good reasons in this monetary sphere for not being afraid of some concentration.

Whatever the links between the centre and the intermediaries, the collection of information, the information required, can never be perfect. The system will still be subject to shocks; things will happen which no one, who was in a position to take action, had foreseen. It is a system which is based upon arrangements for risk-taking in the face of an uncertain future; as such it is bound to be fragile. An arm's length system is particularly fragile. A serious blow to one part of it can have wide repercussions. Closer association, by making it easier to find a 'lender of last resort', reduces the fragility.

13 Interest and Investment

The post-Wicksellian models, with which we have been dealing in the preceding chapter, have been concerned with the transmission of signals from the centre to the 'circumference' of the monetary or financial system; their effects on the 'real' economy, outside that system, have been left unexplored. Wicksell's preoccupation with long-run equilibrium made it hard for him to have anything useful to say on this matter; Keynes was not troubled by that obstacle, but there was another which, as we shall see, got in his way. There are ideas which have come up since the time of Keynes which give more help.

They can best be introduced by some consideration of a theory which was available to Keynes and which he is well known to have rejected—rightly if it is taken as he understood it, but if he had looked round to see what could be made of it, not so rightly. This is that which is associated with the name of his contemporary, R. G. Hawtrey.[1] Hawtrey's *Currency and Credit* appeared in 1919; so it may be reckoned to have been a standard work on monetary theory in the decade before Keynes's *Treatise*. It was Hawtrey's doctrine that the principal way in which interest affects trade activity is through its effects on speculative markets in commodities. I have given a sketch of the working of such a market in Chapter 2. I have no reason to suppose that either Hawtrey or Keynes would have disagreed with it. It appeared that in such a market, positive quantities of stock being held, current price would tend to equal expected price for some future date, minus cost of holding to that date; and in that cost, interest would be a constituent part. Thus if the expected price was given, a rise in rate of interest (here, presumably, a *short* rate of interest closely tied to central bank rate) would cause a fall in current price in correspondence. We may call this the *arithmetical* Hawtrey effect; it was this that most of his readers in the twenties, Keynes in particular, thought him to have had in mind. If that had been all, it looked easy to crush it. No more need be said than what Keynes said in the *Treatise*:[2]

[1] I shall be drawing on my paper on Hawtrey in *Economic Perspectives* (1977).
[2] *Treatise*, Volume 1, pp. 194–5.

[Hawtrey relies] exclusively on the increased costs of business resulting from dearer money. [He] admits that these additional costs will be too small materially to affect the manufacturer, but assumes without investigation that they do materially affect the trader. He does not base his argument on the arousing of an expectation of falling price-levels in the minds of the dealers. . . . Yet probably the question whether he is paying 5 or 6 per cent for the accommodation he receives from his banker influences the mind of the dealer very little more than it influences the mind of the manufacturer, as compared with the current and prospective rate of off-take for the goods he deals in and his expectations as to their prospective price-movements.

So, for Keynes and subsequently for Keynesians, that was that!

Hawtrey however did not admit that he was defeated; in subsequent works[3] he returned to the charge. Chiefly he maintained that there was much historical evidence, which he assembled in detail, to show that changes in bank rate had, or often had, much more influence on markets than Keynes would allow. (It should be noticed that this evidence largely related to the period of what was in Chapter 11 called the old trade cycle.) For this he had an explanation, in what he called 'psychological factors'. That was a bad term, but a better has since been discovered. The issue was one of the *rationality* of expectations.

Neither he nor Keynes disputed that 'expectation of prospective price-movements' is a dominant influence on speculative markets. But how are such expectations formed? There were at first sight two alternatives. Either they are based on information, available in the present, or they are quite random. Close-up observation of markets led Keynes to prefer the latter alternative; markets so often appeared to move in ways that no one could explain. Speculation, on this view, is just a gamble. A 'herd instinct' would be invoked to account for the phenomenon of bull and bear markets. But, Hawtrey might rejoin (though I don't think he did so explicitly), are these necessarily indications of irrationality?

For suppose one regards perfect rationality and perfect irrationality as two extremes, leaving plenty of room for something in between. Rational expectations must be based on information; but the information may be good, or much less than is required. Or it may be good in some directions but deficient in others. (In terms of my 'harvest' example in Chapter 2, the date at which better information about a forthcoming harvest would be available could be known

[3] Chiefly in *A Century of Bank Rate* (1939).

fairly exactly; that would be a help to the stockholder, but by no means all he would like to have.) That is the kind of thing I mean by rational choice on imperfect information.

We can thus admit that if relevant information is hard to come by, the market may well approximate to what Keynes called it—a 'casino'. If the most that is available to the individual operator is to notice what others are doing, the 'herd' phenomenon could be explained, without abandoning rationality altogether. Short-run expectations would then be formed from extrapolation of current price-movements; in a fluid market, from which it is easy to extract oneself if one makes a mistake, it may be quite rational to proceed in that way. But even so, it would be rational to change one's expectation on the receipt of new information; and Keynes did elsewhere admit that this might happen. A change in bank rate, he said himself, may 'constitute a new fact—by throwing new light on the policy and intentions of the monetary authority'.[4] That really gives Hawtrey what he needs; as he put it,[5]

When the use of bank rate to restrict credit became an established practice, traders, being aware of the intentions of the Bank, were inclined to anticipate them. When bank rate went up from 3 to 4 per cent, a trader would reason that this was intended to have a restrictive effect on markets, and that, if the effect was not brought about, the rate would simply go higher and higher until it was.

So, if a rise in bank rate was taken in such a way, and in such conditions, that it would be taken to be intended to have a decisive effect, it would have that effect, even though the arithmetical effect which could be calculated to follow from it was small.

I therefore conclude, in spite of Keynes, that Hawtrey's channel is one of the channels along which a change in monetary policy, expressed as a change in central bank rate, *may* take effect. In the days of the old cycle, to which most of Hawtrey's examples refer, it could well have been a major channel; in latter days, when so many commodity markets are managed in the interests of producers, it is less impressive, at least if taken literally. It should however be noticed (as Hawtrey himself observed) that when currencies are floating, speculation on foreign exchanges works in a similar manner. A rise in central bank rate in a single country, if it is taken decisively, has its

    4 *Treatise*, Volume 1, p. 202.
    5 *Century*, p. 279.

most unmistakeable effect on the external value of that country's currency. Effects on commodity markets are mixed up with that. And there is no question that a definite change in the exchange rate has an effect, at least on industries that are exposed to foreign competition.

Hawtrey's own precept was not for unlimited floating, but for floating about a parity, which was to be kept at least relatively firm. That in his view would retain a good part of the controllability of the old cycle. It is effectively the arrangement which has been formalized in the constitution of the European system (EMS). So, granted this interpretation, the Hawtrey channel would appear to have survived.

I turn to consider the other channel, which plays a corresponding part in the work of Keynes. This was a matter of the impact of the (long) rate of interest on fixed capital investment. It will prove to have been useful to approach it, as I have been doing, from consideration of his controversy with Hawtrey, since it can hardly be doubted that this was the route along which Keynes was led to it. He had shown to his own satisfaction, that the Hawtrey effect was not strong enough to bear the weight that Hawtrey had laid upon it. As I showed, this objection ran in terms of its calculated arithmetical effect. Keynes had no difficulty in showing that in the case of investment in fixed capital the arithmetical effect would be larger.

It will however be useful to have some figures in mind. Take a rise in interest from 5 to 6 per cent, such as both of our authors appear to have been considering. A Hawtreyan merchant, planning to sell at the end of six months, and perfectly confident of the price at which he would be selling, would reduce his current demand price in the ratio of $97\frac{1}{2}$ to 97, approximately, that is, by $\frac{1}{2}$ per cent. A Keynesian manufacturer supposing (a very extreme case!) that he thought his machine would last for ever, and was confident that it would go on yielding the same return, would reduce his demand price in the ratio of 1 to 6, nearly 17 per cent. But that sets weight on what is to happen in the distant future, to an extent which is quite ridiculous. A similar calculation, with the machine expected to last for no more than ten years, seems to result in a fall of about 5 per cent. That is more reasonable, and it could be sufficient for Keynes.

It would nevertheless have been desirable to ask: how much of industrial investment would fit into anything like that pattern? Perhaps the most promising case is that of the 'speculative' builder of dwelling-houses, houses which he will let out for rent. The value to him of a completed house could then be taken to be the capitalized value of the stream of rents which he would charge. Houses being quite durable, this would be fairly sensitive to changes in the (long) rate of interest. The same would hold, in a slightly more complicated manner, if the house is to be sold to its prospective occupier, who has raised the money to pay for it on a mortgage. A reduction in the interest rate, making a mortgage loan easier to get and to pay for, would surely stimulate the demand for new houses. (This was in fact the most obvious effect, in the 1930s in England, of the reduction in interest which actually occurred at the time when Keynes was writing. There was a boom in the construction of private residential houses.)

There is however a general principle which in this latter case already comes up. A person who raises the money to buy a house which he is himself to live in, whether by borrowing on mortgage or by selling securities he had been owning, puts himself in a less liquid position; so a question of liquidity comes in here, no less than in the financial markets. The loss of liquidity is moderated if the house that has been bought can readily be resold. It is thus of much importance that facility of borrowing does not only increase the demand for new houses; it has a similar effect on already existing houses; but greater activity in the market for such houses makes a house a less illiquid asset, so as well as the direct there is this indirect effect.

Though there are some durable instruments employed in industry for which much the same is true as is true in the case of dwelling-houses (transport vehicles are perhaps a leading example), it is surely more common for the instrument to be associated with an existing, or planned, process of production. It is expected to play a part in that process of production; it is much more valuable in that place than it could be in any alternative use. The price that the firm is prepared to pay for it will then be hardly affected by what could be got for it on resale. The 'machine' is a single member of a bundle of complements. Two quite different problems of choice then make their appearance, according to whether the investment is *defensive* or *innovative*.

We shall need a definition of this distinction. Every investment in capital goods has to be paid for, so its effect on the balance-sheet of the firm undertaking it has two sides. On the one hand there is the acquisition of the good, a new asset; on the other a new liability, or the giving-up of a financial asset. Whichever way the expenditure is financed, there is on that side a loss of liquidity, an increase in exposure to risk;[6] this will naturally be less formidable if the funds can be got on easy terms. But the corresponding effect on the other side may go either way. There are some kinds of investment in fixed capital which diminish in this direction the riskiness of the firm's position; these I call defensive investment. There are some which increase it; these I call innovative.

The simplest kind of defensive investment is mere replacement. The new 'machine' takes the place of a predecessor that is worn out, or is wearing out. Whether or not to replace will not often be affected by interest, or by the terms on which funds can be raised; the gain from having the whole plant in proper working order must usually outweigh any interest cost on a particular machine. A change in interest may indeed affect the date at which the new machine is ordered. At a high rate of interest it may well pay to hang on longer with an appliance that is bound in the end to be condemned. But to attach much importance to that sort of saving is hardly symptomatic of good business management.

That interest does not have much to do with pure problems of replacement is I think widely accepted; but it is not so often noticed that the same holds much more widely. Any existing process of production may be in need of reinforcement, for other reasons than physical wearing-out. So there are many kinds of defensive investment. Some may arise from a desire to improve relations with labour employed, which have been deteriorating; facilities provided to improve 'working conditions' are quite likely to require some capital expenditure. Most important are those which arise from competition. The introduction of a new technique we should reckon as innovative, in the case of the firm which first introduces it; but it is defensive, in the firms which find themselves threatened by its competition, and must follow in order not to be left behind. They must follow, whatever the cost, or drop out of the race.

The effect of interest on each kind of defensive investment thus seems unlikely to be considerable.

I accordingly turn to innovative investment,[7] where there are three types to be distinguished. In all of them, quite apart from the loss of liquidity involved in the capital expenditure, there is increased exposure to risk. It is difficult to think of any such increase in ex-

---

[6] See Appendix on risk and uncertainty.

[7] I have been helped in writing this section by the book of Amendola and Gaffard, *The Innovative Choice* (1988), which came into my hands as I was starting to write it.

posure which does not involve the construction of a new plant (or department of plant); so I shall take it that that is always involved. The plant has to be constructed (and that takes time) before it can be used. So there is a construction period and a utilization, or running, period which need to be distinguished. It is in the running period that the gain, which is the incentive to make the innovation, must ordinarily be expected to accrue. My three types are classified according to the form in which it is expected (or hoped) that it will accrue.

In Type A, which may perhaps be regarded as the most innovative, there is not only a new plant but a new product to be produced from it—a product that has not been produced by anyone before. Here there are not only risks on the production side, of neither construction nor running coming out as intended; there are also risks on the side of selling the product, of finding a demand for it.

In Type B there is no change in the character of the product; the gain is expected to come from an increase[8] in capacity to produce it.

In Type C there is again no change in character of product but also no change in planned output of it. The gain from the installation of the new plant must be entirely a matter of reduction in running costs.

With these three types in our minds, each may be looked at further, in comparison with the others.

The risks involved in investment of Type A, considered in general, are very formidable. It faces not only the production risks, which are common to all our Types, but also selling risks arising in a form which makes them particularly hard to judge. The best information about saleability must often come from experience (of somebody) with a similar product. The more similar, the better the information; but also the more similar, the harder it must be to break into the market. Thus to start a project of Type A, on at all a large scale, must usually be intolerably risky. What happens in practice is to start with a small-scale *pilot plant*, which is not expected to be profitable, taken by itself; the object in constructing it is not direct pursuit of profit, it is 'testing the water', gaining information. It is like an experiment in natural science.

Success of the experiment gives evidence (not necessarily conclusive evidence) that it can be profitable to repeat it, on a larger scale. That is to say, it prepares for an investment of Type B. So, from the point of view of the economist, the two may just as well be taken to-

---

[8] It must be an *increase* in capacity, for if the new plant is to have a smaller capacity, its output could be produced from the old plant, so the gain falls under C.

gether. The experiment may be reckoned as part of the constructional stage of the A + B investment. It lengthens out this
constructional stage, leaving the utilizational stage of B as that at
which it is hoped to make a profit.

The whole project (A + B) will have a time-scale that is quite considerable. Our entrepreneur, as we may now call him, will not want
to be obliged to carry his calculations forward into the distant
future—to the distant date at which the equipment may still be expected to be in physical working order—for by that time, he will say,
'anything may happen.' It is the nearer future to which he will want
to look. During that time his capital expenditure, beginning low, will
build up to a peak and then decline. While it is declining, a stream of
receipts, on the other side of his account, will start to come in and
then (it is hoped) build up to a steady level. As I have said, he will not
want to lay much stress on that last stage; he is likely to be more concerned with the prior question—can he get by so as to reach those
calmer waters? The peak of his exposure may well come after the
peak of the capital expenditure; for though that is declining, the
receipts which are to offset it have hardly started. So the great question for him concerns his liquidity, at the point when he is in sight of
his big output, and can begin to have confidence (of which he can
persuade his banker) in his ability to go on selling it.

It is easy to see, in the light of this approach, why testing a project
in terms of the length of time which will have to be taken for it to
'pay for itself' is popular in business. It is a way of approximating to
the true test—the calculation of the balance-sheet, as it is likely to be
at various dates after the project is undertaken, and considering
whether the finance involved is likely to be forthcoming. I have personal experience of a firm which did make its decisions in that latter
manner, and did so successfully.

A project cannot be started in the middle; and it would rarely be
advantageous to stop it in the middle, however high the rate of interest rises. So it is the effect of interest rate on the starting of projects
about which we have mainly to think. If the entrepreneur is thinking
in the manner just described, what would chiefly matter to him
would be the state of his balance-sheet at the time of maximum exposure; this at the start may be quite a way ahead. He can be surer of
being protected on that occasion if he finances the plan by borrowing
long, or by issue of shares; but that means raising funds which will
not for some time be spent. Thus, although it may be accepted that in

this case a fall in interest, provided it gets through to easier conditions for industrial borrowing, is conducive to capital investment, the effect on that investment may be considerably delayed.

I turn in conclusion to my Type C. This may be more straightforward. For if no change in final output is being planned, the only gain that can be expected from having the new plant is a reduction in running costs. If the running inputs required for the one plant and for the other are fairly similar in character, the gain should be calculable by technical experts, perhaps fairly firmly. The flow of returns which may be expected from the capital expenditure should thus be calculable, and the effect of a change in interest should be straightforward. It should be nearly as clear as in the case of building houses. There are however two qualifications which have to be made.

One is that if the inputs required on the one plan and on the other are notably different, a change in their relative prices—at the stage of decision, a change in their future relative prices—can be upsetting. The change may appear to be profitable at current relative prices; but what if, during the lifetime of the project, they should change? Coal-firing and oil-firing is obviously a leading example. Uncertainty about such relative prices, as they will be in the future, is obviously a deterrent to Type C investment, whatever happens to interest rates.

The other, assuming that the former does not arise, is that this is precisely the case of the 'machinery effect' of Ricardo. During the construction period, while the old plant is still in operation, there must be a net increase in demand for labour, the labour employed in the construction being added to the unchanged employment on the old. But afterwards, when the new plant takes the place of the old, its construction phase being over, there must be a net diminution in demand, even with respect to what it was before the construction started. So if progress is to be maintained at all smoothly, and all innovation is of this character, there must be a succession of such investments, as (in effect) Ricardo saw.

Though the point was so well made by Ricardo, neither 'neo-classics' nor Keynesians gave it much attention. I may claim that in my own work, especially in my later work, I have gone on attending to it, in several ways.[9]

[9] It is possible to state it in a 'neo-classical' manner, but only in terms of a three-factor production function (old capital, new capital, and labour). The great neoclassics were not very good at that, but it can be done. (See my chapter on the production function, at the end of *Capital and Time*; also the new paper on 'Elasticity of substitution', in the third volume of my *Collected Essays*.)

14 An International Economy

As I have throughout insisted, this is a theoretical book; its concluding chapters will be no less theoretical than the others. There have
however been practical questions to which some of them may have
had relevance; one to which this may have relevance is very topical.
Should Britain enter, or not enter, or partly enter, the European
Monetary System (EMS)? I shall not attempt any direct answer to
that question. I shall confine myself to the construction of a theoretical model, which may have a bearing upon it—and on similar questions which have come up in the past, and will surely continue to do
so, as far ahead as one can look.

Thus what I am to mean by an international economy is one consisting of a number of national economies, each of which uses its
own money. Within each nation are a number (which we take to be
a large number) of separate decision-makers, persons and firms,
private and public, which have commercial and financial relations
between them. The parties to a transaction may have the same, or
they may have different, national attachments. The significance of
the national money is that it is used (we take it that legal arrangements compel it to be used) as standard of value in internal transactions; but for external transactions, where the parties belong to
different nations, no such rule can be laid down. The contract which,
as we saw in Chapter 5, must in general precede delivery must be
expressed in terms of some money, acceptable to both parties; that
may be the money of one party or of the other, or some third money
on which the two may more easily agree.[1] But whichever way it is
adopted, a market between currencies, on which one money is
exchanged for another, has to be brought in before the bargain can
be completed. It will be assumed, in nearly all cases that I shall be
considering, that such a market exists.

It is conceivable that a country might insist that all exports from it
should be invoiced in its own currency; but that does not often
happen, for what would be the point of imposing such a restriction?
The contract sets up a debt from importer to exporter; if there were to

---

[1] It is sufficient in this context to confirm attention to bilateral transactions.

be trouble in collecting it, it would be in the law of his own country that a claim against him would have to be pursued, if it needed to be pursued. To insist that the debt must be expressed in terms of the exporter's own currency must make exporting more difficult, to no advantage. To insist that imports should be invoiced in terms of the domestic currency is a possible form of protectionism; but from the point of view of the protectionist, it is not an attractive alternative. We may therefore assume that the choice of currency in which the debt is to be expressed is left to be agreed on by the trading parties themselves. Each will have some objection to the use of the other's currency, so it is very likely that it will be some third currency, in which each has some confidence, that they will choose to use. It might not be the same currency which was used in this way throughout the whole international economy; sterling area, dollar area, French franc area, rouble area, have certainly in practice been heard of. But we may surely allow ourselves, for the purpose of our model, to accept that it is just one currency which in this way is generally used. A model that is constructed in this way will surely fit, not too badly, a good many historical, and contemporary, facts.

Accordingly, in the model, there are two kinds of currency, and two kinds of country corresponding. All countries but one have two currencies that concern them, their own and the international; that one however has only one currency, for the international money is also its domestic. It will surely be understood, once this is realized, that monetary problems and policies look quite different according as they are regarded from the standpoint of the 'central' country, or from that of one of the others.

Most of what I shall be saying will turn on this distinction, so it will be a help to give the countries names. I do not wish to rush on to contemporary identifications, so I must invent the names. I thus propose to call the *central* country (the currency of which, in Bretton Woods jargon, would have been called the 'key' currency) *Centralia*, and its money correspondingly the *cent*. It has not been so easy to find suitable names for the other countries and their currencies; but the following, though at first sight surprising, should be easy to remember. When I want to turn round and look at the system from the point of view of one particular non-central country, I shall call its money, correspondingly, the *penny*; *Penland* will then do as the name of the country where pennies are the domestic money. This has the advantage that any non-central country can be called a *land*; other lands than Penland will just be *Otherlands*. Otherlands of course do not have a common currency.

Every country may be supposed to have a banking system; but since we shall not be concerned with the internal structure of that banking system, we may take it to be fully integrated—all banking business, within that country, is performed by that single bank. But we had better not suppose that the bank has a monopoly of dealings in foreign exchange. We can allow other people and businesses in Penland to hold cents as well as pennies (including claims in these denominations) so that a free market can develop between them. The Penland bank may buy or sell on that market; but it cannot sell cents unless it has a stock of cents from which to sell. It can 'create' pennies if it chooses to do so; so it is only by its supply of cents that it is constricted.

If its supply of cents is ample, it can 'peg' the rate of exchange, selling them when their price on the market rises above a desired level, buying them when it falls lower. If the peg is perfect, the exchange rate being completely stabilized, the only source from which the Penland bank could acquire cents would be Penland exporters, except in so far as there was explicit borrowing of cents from non-Penlanders (either Centralians or Otherlanders). Subject to a corresponding qualification, the only reason why cents should be withdrawn from the bank would be to pay for imports—imports from any country, since all alike would have to be paid for in cents. Thus, subject again to these qualifications, the bank's reserve of cents will rise, during a period, by the amount of the country's balance of payments, if that is favourable; or fall if it is adverse. This can continue unless, as a result of a continuing adverse balance, the bank's reserve falls so low that convertibility, at the pegged rate, is threatened.

If this happens there are of course two alternatives which are open to Penland (its bank or the government which stands behind it) on its own initiative to take. On the one hand, it may be possible to take direct measures to improve the current balance. Whatever form these take, whether fiscal or monetary, they must nearly inevitably imply a restriction of imports, for it is easier to work on the import side than on the export.[2] On the other hand, the peg may be withdrawn; the bank ceases to operate on the market for foreign

---

[2] That devaluations are often followed, rather immediately, by an expansion of exports (as the econometrists observe) only shows that the devaluation had been expected.

exchange; the exchange is allowed to 'find its own level'. There are some things which need to be said about each of these alternatives.

First, it is unlikely that there will be any action, not completely disruptive, which will quickly restore the current import–export balance. Even the most drastic restrictions on imports will take time to take effect, if only because those coming up to be paid for have been contracted for in advance; the contract must be carried out, if there is not to be a default on it. Taxes on imports are bound to take time to exercise their full effect, since the domestically produced goods which are (at least in part) to replace them take time to produce. Thus the authorities will be well advised to take steps before they are compelled to do so. If they have not done so, a gap is left which must be filled in some other way.

A depreciation of the exchange will also take time to affect the current balance; but this is one of the cases where speculation can be a help (see Chapters 2 and 13). Non-Penlanders, as we have seen, have no reason for holding pennies as a transaction balance; but they can have a speculative demand for them, if they expect their value, in terms of cents, to be going to recover. This should prevent their value on the market, in terms of cents, from falling indefinitely. With this assistance, slowly acting remedies can be given time to take effect.

It is important however to realize that what is in principle the same alleviation can occur without a depreciation in the external value of the currency, by a rise in the rate of interest on short loans that is offered by the bank. This will have internal effects, within the country, which will react on the current balance; but that effect also, for similar reasons, is likely to be slow (see again Chapter 13). If however it is open to foreigners to lend (to the Penland bank or to other Penlanders) at these high rates of interest, taking them to be higher than can easily be got in other countries, there can be a (temporary) movement of funds towards Penland, purchase of pennies by non-Penlanders, which in favourable conditions can go a long way towards filling the gap.

It must however be emphasized, emphatically emphasized, that the effectiveness of these alternatives, either of these alternatives, depends on a minimum degree of confidence in the stability of the currency (of the value of the penny in terms of the cent) being maintained. If that confidence is lost, neither will work. It is only if it is expected that the penny will recover to its normal level or near it that there can be an incentive to speculate on its recovery; and it is only if there is confidence that the peg will be held that it can be defended by the offer of a high rate of interest in terms of pennies, which is all that the Penland bank—without external support, not yet mentioned—is able to offer. Thus while a pegged rate can readily be defended against moderate and not long-lasting disturbances, its longer-run stability depends on flexibility of internal prices and wages, or on the absence of any disturbance which will lead to a continuing adverse balance, when there is inflexibility.

I do not think that this principle is greatly modified if one brings in the possibility of external support, as from a world bank or some such institution. In terms of our model, this would amount to borrowing from the Centralian bank. The loan would be expressed in cents, as it would suit each party for it to be; and it would be natural for the lender to insist that repayment of it, and interest upon it, should also be expressed in cents. But if the borrower is to make a credible promise to make such payments, he must show that he is taking steps to remedy the present weakness of his position, steps in which the lender can be induced to have some belief. This can easily be represented as putting himself under the tutelage of the lender. Tutelage tends to be resented: more bitterly resented, in this international case, than in the basically corresponding internal case, where (as we have seen in Chapter 7) a weak bank may find a way out from its troubles by entering into dependence on a stronger bank. Thus while as reinforcement to other means of dealing with a temporary emergency, borrowing from an international agency may well have a useful function, for dealing with more deep-rooted troubles the economic dependency which it implies can hardly be prevented from revealing itself as political.

I turn to consider, in corresponding terms, or in terms that shall be as near as possible corresponding, the case of Centralia itself. If Centralia has an adverse balance, it has to pay out cents; but the supply of cents is under its own control. The value of the cent is pegged at unity, whatever anyone does about it. So it is only in terms of something else that it can conceivably be pegged.

Various plans for such pegging will doubtless come to the mind of the readers; for are they not what discussions of international monetary policy are commonly all about? I shall not venture to say much about them. It is more to the point in this place to attend to the prior question: what is to happen if there is no such peg?

In its absence, if the monetary policy of Centralia is entirely passive, adjustment is left to be made by the other countries, the *lands* in the terminology we have been using. If Centralia is running a surplus on its current balance (not matched by loans which its people are deliberately making to landers) some of the lands must be running deficits; the means that are open to them for dealing with those deficits have been discussed. Though the problem in this case is more global than that we were discussing, it does not appear to be of different character. It is the other case, of a Centralia deficit, on which there is more to be said.

If Centralia is running a deficit (again not covered by deliberate borrowing) there must be at least some lands where bank reserves are rising; but their banks are not obliged to take steps to deal with their situation, apart from paying out domestic currency in exchange for the cents their exporters will have earned. Let us consider the position of one such country, which (since it is the one of the lands to which we now desire to direct particular attention) we may call Penland, as before. And we may for the moment confine ourselves to relations between Penland and Centralia. The Centralian deficit is matched by a Penland surplus.

When the issue is posed in this manner, it should set us asking: how could the deficit have come about? There would seem to be two principal possibilities which need to be distinguished, ways in which a condition of deficit could succeed a former condition of balance. On the one hand there might have been an improvement in the efficiency of production in Penland relative to Centralia, so that Penland's exports have become more competitive with Centralia's exports, or are displacing domestically produced goods on the home (Centralian) market. Though if this happened there would be a stage in the process which would show up as a balance-of-payment deficit, it would be (at least technically) 'self-correcting'. There would be a 'deflation' of spending in Centralia and an 'inflation' in Penland—an adjustment which in the Centralian case might be highly disagreeable, but which, if neither country was producing to capacity, might not be reflected in a significant change in consumer prices, other than of those where the effect was direct (such as exports from Penland to Centralia).

The other way in which a Centralian deficit might come about would be an increased demand by Centralians for Penland goods, which could happen independently of any change in production costs. The most interesting case of this is when it is engineered by an expansionary policy of the Centralian government, which (since the supply of cents is under its own control) is not obliged by external constraint to balance its budget—in any sense. We have seen that in the absence of such policy, an increase in competitive pressure from Penland would lead to contraction in Centralia; there could then be pressure for this to be offset by an expansion in public expenditure. (A 'Keynesian' policy, whatever it was called!) In so far as the expenditure was on Centralian products, it would go to offset the contraction in Centralia which would have occurred without it; but some (directly or indirectly) must spill over into imports, thus resulting in expansion or 'inflation' outside. If (as at this point it would be proper to do) we extend our model to admit the existence of a number of *lands* (non-Centralian countries) there could well be some for which the expansion was very welcome, while there could be others, who were having difficulty in controlling their own inflationary tendencies, to whom it would not be welcome at all. It is true that they could in principle protect themselves by revaluing their currencies in terms of cents; but that, for a country which (by assumption) was already in a difficult position, could well appear to be a dangerous course to take.

It thus appears that when a number of countries are trading together, and the currency of one of them is accepted to be the international currency—this may happen, as we have seen, through 'market forces', without any treaty having been needed to establish it—the others may be subjected to 'imported' deflation or inflation coming from the central country, even when in that central country there is neither (its price-level being fairly stable).

Against this background, we may consider the question: is there any device by which the central country could be taken down from its privileged position, so that the choice of policies facing the various countries could be made more similar, or as one might say equalized? Surely, as a matter of historical experience, such a device has existed; it was the Gold Standard. It was then believed that a currency (whether central or not) was bound to be more secure if its value could be kept fixed, or nearly fixed, in terms of some 'hard' or nonfinancial commodity, acceptable in each country; that selected, chiefly for historical reasons which need not here concern us, was gold. It could however have been any other commodity, which satisfied the necessary conditions for a speculative market in it to be possible (see Chapter 2). Since gold is not subject to physical deterioration when it is stocked, it is indeed particularly suitable for that purpose; another commodity could however have been used, though with a little more trouble. We should thus be thinking of the government of each country setting up a department, associated with its bank, committed to stabilizing the price of gold in the national currency, buying and selling gold for national currency, so as to keep the price of gold in that currency at the level desired. If its supply of gold was threatening to run out, it would take steps to draw funds from other countries, using them to acquire gold on the markets of those other countries—the regular Gold Standard proceeding!

It is useful to notice that such an arrangement is not inconsistent with the currencies of one of the countries being *central*, in the sense of our previous discussion. International transactions could be carried on in terms of that currency, not in terms of gold. Nevertheless it would be particularly important, for the maintenance of the Standard, that the gold price, in terms of that central currency, should be held firm. Other currencies might be allowed to 'find their levels'; but if the central currency was firmly based, the system would possess a firm international money.

This was the system which did indeed operate—broadly, though of course with complications of detail—not so badly[3] for nearly a century before 1914. Throughout that epoch, it was sterling which most nearly played the part of our central currency. That this was so was dramatically demonstrated by an event which took place at the end of it, at the moment of declaration of war in 1914. On the day war was declared, the Bank of England raised its Bank Rate from 4 to 10 per cent, reckoning, it is to be supposed, that what was then a scarifyingly high rate would be needed to hold the funds of non-belligerents in London. But before a week had elapsed, it was brought down to 5 per cent, nearly where it was before. For the expected drain had not eventuated.[4] I think this can be interpreted as an indica-

---

[3] Its ability to accommodate itself to exogenous change in flow demand and supply for gold (such as the hoarding by the new German government after 1870 and the new South African suppliers in the nineties) is surely remarkable; it had more elasticity than is commonly supposed.

[4] See the account by J. H. Clapham, which (originally written for a planned third volume of his history of the Bank in the eighteenth and nineteenth centuries), is now available as an appendix to the continuation carried out by R. S. Sayers (Volume 3, pp. 31–45).

tion that even then sterling was something of a *centre*. And since it was expected that the war would not be long continuing, it would continue so to act.

That expectation of course was falsified. What destroyed the centrality of sterling, as the war continued, was the imposition, inevitable in the circumstances, of exchange control by the British Government, which brought the free market, in gold and in foreign exchange, to an end. So when more or less free trading resumed, after the war, the markets had to find another centre, and they found it hard to find one.

A word may perhaps be said, in concluding this historical digression, about the abortive British 'return to the Gold Standard' of 1925; it has more significance, from a modern perspective, than is commonly supposed. Keynes taught his contemporaries to look at it from an *internally* British point of view; it has since been generally accepted that from that point of view at the gold value selected the pound was overvalued. The General Strike of 1926, and the long coal-miners' strike that was associated with it, are pointed to as evidence. It can however be maintained on the other side that trouble in coal-mining was inevitable, whatever the rate of exchange that had been fixed; it was due to the resumption of German exports, in the absence of which British coal-miners had been able to establish a level of wages which was now unsustainable. Apart from that special trouble, the return of 1925 did not, for five years or so, do so badly. Progress was made towards at least a partial resumption of sterling centrality. Could even so much have been done if a lower parity had been selected, as Keynes advocated? The prestige of the old parity must have facilitated resumption, on the international front.

Nevertheless the episode is worth recalling, since it marked a subsequently influential emergence of the clash between monetary policies, directed on the one hand to internal and on the other to external stability, a clash that is still with us today.

I do not have the empirical knowledge to continue, even in this vein, with the later story, so must proceed to sum up. The most appropriate way of doing so may be to examine what *precepts* (to succeed the Thornton Gold Standard precepts: see Chapter 11) appear to follow from what I have been saying. But even that is no simple matter.

For it cannot now be expected that the rules will be the same for all sorts of countries, fitting for any situation in which a particular country may find itself. We must at the least distinguish between the central and non-central countries; but that is not enough. We also need to distinguish between those which have strong and those that have weak currencies—using *strong* and *weak* in senses which correspond to strength and weakness in the case of banks. Thus a country would have a strong currency if there was confidence in the unlikelihood of occasions arising when crisis measures would have to be taken to defend it. It was balancing, and expected to go on balancing, its external payments; or it might have a regular balance in its favour, giving it surplus funds it could invest abroad. If for a while it had an unfavourable balance, it had reserves on which it could draw, or it could borrow on its excellent credit. A weak currency would continually need to be supported, and supporting it would always be a problem.

Centrality and strength do not necessarily go together. Centrality is not acquired by a decision of the 'central' government, or of its banking system; it comes from decisions by others, who choose to make the currency of that country their chief 'international'. No doubt it is unlikely that such a choice would have been made unless the central currency, at the time it became *central*, had been a strong currency; but it could continue to be central, having no obvious rival, even when it was losing its strength. So there are several cases which fall to be considered, the chief division being between those where the strength of the central currency in unquestioned, and those where it is in doubt.

In the former cases, while the central currency is (by definition) a strong currency, those of the others may be strong or may be weak. It is tempting to say that the monetary problems of these non-central currencies can then be treated separately, by expansionary policies in the stronger, contractionary in the weaker; or if the internal consequences (on employment or 'inflation') are unwelcome, by an upward or downward revaluation of their rates of exchange. Most of the obstacles in the way of such measures are familiar, and need not be specified. It should however be emphasized that it is no solution, not a way in which a country with a weak currency can easily get out of its difficulty, just to float its exchange. For a floating rate will just continue to fall unless an expectation can be aroused that from some point in the fall it will recover. Thus it is safer to devalue, to a rate which is planned to be held and which is intended to be defended, than just to let go. There are many countries which have had, and have, bitter experiences in that direction. Nevertheless it is clear what should be done, though it may be hard to do it.

The problems of the central currency are more peculiar. So long as it is of unquestioned strength (as the pound sterling was before 1914 and the US dollar was in the 1960s) its country can afford to base its monetary policy on internal considerations, thinking of itself as if it were a closed economy, and acting accordingly. Its actions, though internally oriented, will indeed have external repercussions; in an extreme case these may react back on the centre, as happened in 1930–3. A Thornton precept, as we have seen in Chapter 11, could in such a case have stood up well. The 'devaluation' of the dollar in 1933, by the incoming administration of Franklin Roosevelt, can in these terms be defended as necessary, in those still partially Gold Standard days, as a preliminary to the expansionary policies that were called for, both in the US and outside it.

The floating of the dollar in 1973 would appear, from this point of view, to be a sad contrast. It is most readily to be interpreted as an attempt by the American authorities to abdicate from the central responsibilities that had fallen upon them. But, as we have seen, it is not in the power of a single government to disclaim such responsibilities. This became clear after a year or two. The abdication was not accepted. The dollar remained the central currency; it was accepted as such throughout the trading world; but it no longer commanded the former confidence. That meant, consequentially, that non-US countries, seeking to stabilize the external values of their currencies, had no standard by which they could judge what was stable. They were themselves thrown back to working, in the first place, for internal stability; but that is itself hard to attain if some degree of external does not go with it.

It would appear that there followed a stage when the Americans realized (under President Reagan) that the centrality of the dollar should by them be accepted; and that therefore an adverse balance of payments did not for them much matter. They were able to maintain a fair stability of internal prices, and a high level of employment, conceding that this left the rest of the world 'awash with dollars'. But then, as this continued, the centrality of the dollar came under suspicion. Can another centre be discovered? Or can means be invented by which it would be possible to manage in a stable way without one? I have no means of forming a judgement on such mighty questions.

15 What is Bad about Inflation?

This is a question which at the end of this book, I think I should try to answer. My answer is implied in what I have been saying, but it needs to be set out explicitly.

Economists used to think that they knew the answer, but their old answer will not do. Nevertheless it is convenient to begin with it. I may take it in the form it was stated by Dennis Robertson, in a passage I have often quoted.[1]

> Our economic order is largely based upon the institution of contract ... on the fact, that is, that people enter into binding agreements with one another to perform certain actions at a future date, for a remuneration which is fixed here and now in terms of money. A violent or prolonged change in the value of money saps the confidence with which people make or accept undertakings of this nature.

One can see why Robertson, writing in the 1920s, thought that this was the point to emphasize. He was thinking of an inflation that had started up, after a state of affairs in which prices had been stable, or fairly stable. Contracts had been made on expectation of stable prices; those expectations were cheated by the inflation. There can be no doubt that in those conditions his statement is correct. But his point has less force when inflation has been continuous, so that people have had time to adjust themselves to it. It will then appear that his argument is not an argument for constant prices; it is an argument for reliability. Once inflation has become established, it is indeed an argument against acceleration of inflation. But cannot it then be stood on its head, and used as an argument against deceleration? To impose a condition of non-inflation, upon an economy which has become adjusted to rising prices, would surely, from this point of view, be quite as much of an upset.

I think that the Robertson argument, in this inverted form, does have great weight with contemporary economists. It becomes a doctrine that so long as inflation is 'expected' it does not matter. This is made particularly appealing by the habit many economists have got into of thinking in terms of 'steady state' or 'growth equilibrium'

[1] D. H. Robertson, *Money* (Cambridge Economic Handbooks, 1928 edition, p. 13).

models, in which what happens is what was expected—not that it is claimed that such models are realistic, only that they are manageable. Such a model would behave *in real terms* in just the same way whether the level of money prices was constant or rising quite rapidly. Money rates of interest, being money prices, would have to adjust; but isn't this what happens? The behaviour of the financial markets is indeed captured, on the approach in question, better than that of the rest of the economy.[2]

It was because I wanted to get clear about this, and for my reader to get clear about it, that I decided to start this book with those chapters on the working of markets. They distinguished the ways in which prices are formed on speculative markets—the financial markets are in this sense speculative markets—from the way in which they are increasingly formed on other markets, such as the markets for manufactured goods and the market for labour. On these latter markets, which are surely most important markets, prices have to be 'made' or negotiated; they are not just 'determined' by demand and supply. It is easier to make them, in a way which is acceptable to the parties concerned, because it seems fair, if substantial use can be made of precedent, if one can start with the supposition that what was acceptable before will be acceptable again. When prices in general are fairly stable, that may often be rather easy. The particular prices which result from such bargains may not be ideal from the point of view of the economist; but the time and trouble which would be involved in improving them is not worth while. To be obliged to make them anew, and to go on making them anew, as one is obliged to do in continuous inflation, involves direct economic loss, and very often loss of temper as well.

Any system of prices (a system of railway fares, like a system of wages) has to satisfy economic canons of efficiency and social canons of fairness—canons which it is very difficult to make compatible. So it is hard to re-negotiate it and it saves time not to do this very often. But that means, in an inflationary process, that the prices and wages that are fixed are lagged. Suppose that a wage-system is negotiated

---

[2] If one sticks to this approach but still believes that inflation is bad, one is bound to lay stress upon the cost that is involved, when money rates of interest are high, in holding a balance in the form of non-interest-bearing money; so business will try to manage with less holdings of money even for transaction purposes. There is a loss of convenience in this but it is questionable if it is a major matter. Moreover, in response to the rise in nominal rates on their earning assets, banks will to some extent adjust their deposit rates.

in January, to be revised in the following January. A rate of price-rise of 5 per cent per year is allowed for in fixing it, for that is what has been experienced in the previous year. This compensates for past inflation, but in the current year prices go on rising, while the wage for the moment does not rise. During the year the wage-earner feels himself to be losing ground. If an arrangement such as this continues, he spends most of his time losing ground. Only at the moment of re-fixing does he recover it. No wonder inflation is unpopular with him.

One can see in the light of this why indexation is no answer. It may simplify negotiation at the annual re-fixing, but during the year there will be just the same lag. A way out might perhaps be found by the device which is practised in some countries, of paying only partly in the form of a weekly wage, which is supplemented by a substantial annual bonus. The bonus could be indexed, though the weekly wage was not. But for such a system to be introduced, business must be strong enough, at the point of its introduction, to pay a bonus on top of what they were paying before.

Any general system of wage-indexation raises at its outset most serious problems. It is inevitable, at any particular stage in an inflationary process, that there should be grave disparities in *relative* wages, both social and economic. Are these to be frozen? If not, how are they to be mended? And, even if that first step can be successfully taken, an indexed system will show up its fragility in the event of new shocks, leading to shortages of particular kinds of labour, thus upsetting established relativities.

Indexation just institutionalizes the wage–prices spiral, which is basically the result of defending a level of real wages, or a rate of rise in real wages (or of real incomes, in the broadest sense, which are associated with it) which has become inconsistent with economic realities. That is what happened in Britain in the 1970s, when as a result of the oil shock, and the related rise in the prices of other imports which went along with it, the rise in real wages to which British workers had become accustomed was brought to a sudden halt. That led to wage-inflation; it was the cause of the wage-inflation: monetary policy was just permissive. It is true that it was brought to an end by monetary restriction, which to deal with so great an inflation, never before experienced in peace-time in Britain, had to be savage. Even so, it was slow-acting; so the pain and grief were felt in the first years of Mrs Thatcher's government though the action which led to it had been begun under her predecessor. A democratic Labour government is bound in the end to be anti-inflation.

Was there any way in which there could have been a 'soft landing'? It could only have been done if the real causes which had led to the inflation could have been removed. It is hard to see that the state of mind, the social causes which connect the movement of wages with the movement of prices, could have been changed without a shock. Even the shock which has been given may not have been enough. More hopeful is to work on the other link, from wages to prices. There have been several examples in this century of post-war inflations being brought under control by post-war recovery, recovery of productivity in real terms; as the capital stock of the country recovered, prices would rise more slowly than wages, so the spiral would ease off. As we have seen, the quickest effect of monetary restriction, in a single country, is an improvement in the external value of that country's currency; the 'over-valued' exchange does act as a brake upon the rise in prices, but at the expense of damage to exporting and import-competing industries, with which we are so familiar. The long-run answer must be an improvement in internal productivity, but the damage suffered by these industries makes this harder to attain.

So perhaps what is bad about inflation is principally not its effects—the losses of 'convenience and security' to which older economists gave so much attention—but the weakening of the economy, which is the cause of the evil. If that is cured, inflation, with only a little help from monetary policy, will cure itself.

Something should be said in conclusion about hyper-inflation, the phenomenon of which the leading case was for long the great German inflation of 1923, but of course there are current examples in many parts of the world. I would distinguish this from the moderate inflations of a few percentage points per year which we are learning to live with, not simply by the rate of price rise being so much greater but by the fact that in hyper-inflation no prices can be *established*, for there will be a rise in the price level before any transaction can be completed, so that money is losing its capacity to act as a means of payment. There is a complete or almost complete lack of confidence in the credit of the government.

That confidence cannot be restored by a mere change in denomination—the introduction of a new money in place of the old that is discredited. When that is done and nothing else is done, the new money will just go the way of the old. A way must be found of giving the new money a new credibility.

Here we must distinguish between internal and external credibility. There is one case when external credibility does not matter—when the country can cut itself off from external economic relations, in particular from foreign trade. (Or it may be able to keep some foreign trade by recourse to barter deals, as previously noticed.[3] These must almost inevitably be inter-governmental deals. They require that there should be a pair of countries in a similar monetary position and that each is in a position to offer some of the goods which the other most urgently requires. This is still a modified 'autarky'.)

If the autarky solution in either form is available, it is only internal credibility that has to be restored. That can be done if there is a visible change in government policy, nearly always implying a new government, and a new government that is unlikely to be displaced: A condition that is unlikely to be satisfied by a constitutional government which has to submit itself periodically to re-election.

If that solution—in so far as it is a solution—is rejected, then both internal and external credibility must be restored, and in practice the external comes first, for if external credibility is restored, internal will fairly easily follow. The ways of ensuring that it does are well known. But internal credibility will always be undermined by absence of external. For external to be restored needs support from countries with stronger currency—as was done in the classical German case under the so-called Dawes Plan and Young Plan, without which the new Mark could not have been held. Internal measures were also necessary, but without that external help they could not have succeeded.

So in the modern cases stabilization must be associated in the first case with a clearing up of the foreign debts of the countries affected. And that can hardly be done without putting themselves, for a time, under the financial control of their creditors.

[3] Above, p. 43.

APPENDIX:
RISK AND UNCERTAINTY

The title of this appendix is meant to echo that of the famous book by Frank Knight, *Risk, Uncertainty and Profit* (1920), on which I shall have something important to say before I have concluded. It is something which might not have been uncongenial to him. But I begin with a piece of very formal theory, which would not have appealed to him at all.

It is an exercise in what is called the theory of portfolio selection. I introduce it here, in spite of the very un-Knightian assumptions on which it is based—assumptions I do not much care for myself—because it brings out a point, which in the end does not seem to depend upon them, and which should be quite a help towards understanding what I am saying in this book. So I want to emphasize that my acceptance of these assumptions is only provisional.

We are to consider the behaviour of an operator, who is disposing of a capital of given money value K; he is confronted with opportunities of investing it in some combination of n securities, the current prices of which are given to him, being independent of his own behaviour. There are no transactions costs, so he is not hampered by inheritance from the past; we can think of him as having got the whole of his capital into money form before he decides to invest it. So the whole of his portfolio, after he has made his decision, is that which he has chosen on the basis of the current opportunities open to him.

We think of him having to hold it until a 'week' has elapsed (as in Chapter 2), so it is the *outcome* of his decision, at the end of the week, which he wants to make as favourable as possible to him. But he does not know what the outcome will be. There are possibilities of different outcomes; he has to make his choice with imperfect knowledge of them.

The conventional way of dealing with this problem is to suppose that there are m eventualities, or 'states of the world', any of which may occur. The operator knows what will be the outcome, in each eventuality, of the investment of one unit of money in each security, but he does not know which eventuality will occur. (This just amounts to sweeping the knowns and unknowns into separate boxes.)

Thus if a_{ij} is this known outcome, in the ith eventuality, of a unit of money invested in the jth security, the total outcome of amounts $(x_1, \ldots, x_n)$ to be put into the n securities (among which a non-interest-bearing money may or may not be included) will be

$$y_i = \sum a_{ij} x_j \qquad j = 1, \ldots, n; i = 1, \ldots, m$$

So, corresponding to each vector x of investments in securities, there is a vector y of outcomes in eventualities; but how is the chooser to order them so as to distinguish which he prefers? No advantage is gained from this way of posing the problem unless we give him some criterion by which to do so.

In order to make the outcomes y_i comparable with one another, a means of weighting them is needed; so the next thing to do is to suppose him to attach probabilities to the outcomes, or to the eventualities corresponding. This is what Knight would not allow us to do, on the ground (with which I agree) that the eventualities, important for a portfolio choice such as this, are usually not classifiable; they are not like the results of scientific experiments, where in the long run there will often be a convergence to definite proportions of failure and success.[1] For where, in the field that is here under consideration, shall we find the long-run repetition that is needed? Let us however for the moment forget about that, and suppose that there are *cardinal* probabilities which our operator attaches to his eventualities (p_i with $\sum p_i = 1$).

The simplest scheme of maximization which then presents itself is to suppose that what is maximized is $\sum p_i y_i$, the 'mathematical expectation' of outcome. But that will not do. For

$$\sum p_i y_i = \sum p_i(\sum a_{ij} x_j) = \sum (\sum p_i a_{ij}) x_j$$

and, since $\sum x_j = K$, the operator would just put the whole of his capital into that security for which $\sum p_i a_{ij}$ (the ps and as being independent of his choice) was the largest. Thus, as has been long understood, this solution must be rejected, since it gives no opportunity for spreading of risks.

It was already suggested by the great mathematician Bernoulli, at the beginning of the eighteenth century, that what the chooser should be supposed to maximize is the 'mathematical expectation' of

---

[1] My present view on this matter is set out at length in the chapter entitled 'Probability and judgement' which is appended to my *Causality in Economics* (1979).

the *utility* which he is to derive from his choice. He was writing before there were any utilitarians; but the utility function $u(y)$ which he required had just the properties which have become conventional: that $u'(y)$, the marginal utility (MU), would be positive but would diminish as y increased.

If it is $U = \sum p_i u(y_i)$ which is to be maximized, both the ps and the us must be cardinal numbers. There has been much discussion of cardinal utility, but I do not think that in this place it is relevant. If we accept cardinality for probability, why not for utility? If we do not accept it for probability, the utility question does not arise.

All I shall do with the Bernoulli construction is to see what answer it gives to an interesting question: is there any utility function $u(y)$ which is consistent with a change in K leaving the proportions in which the securities are taken unchanged? It has sometimes been denied that there is any such function; but I think it can be shown that it does exist and is quite instructive.

If all x_j were increased in the same proportion, then all y_i would be increased in the same proportion (assuming of course that the a_{ij} were unchanged). But if the operator were in a preferred position at the old y_i, there must have been a particular relation between their marginal utilities in the old position; it can be shown that this relation will be unchanged when the y_i increase equi-proportionally, if the marginal utilities $u'(y_i)$ also change in equal proportions.[2] Thus, for a small change in K, the *elasticities* of the MU curves $u'(y_i)$ must be the same. But these are not different curves; the different y_i and their corresponding $u'(y_i)$ are different points on the same curve. So what is being said is that the (single) MU curve must have constant elasticity.

Now it is well known that for any downward-sloping curve to have constant elasticity, its equation must be of a particular form. We must have $u'(y) = A y^{-h}$, where A is a constant (positive to keep MU positive) and h is the reciprocal of the Marshallian elasticity. Now the *total* utility corresponding to this is got by integrating with respect to y; in general, this gives

$$\frac{A}{1-h} y^{-h+1} + \text{constant}$$

[2] For let U_j be the expected marginal utility of investment in the jth security. Since each of the coefficients in $K = \sum x_j$ is unity, it will be necessary that in a preferred position, all U_j should be equal. But if $U = \sum p_i u(y_i)$, $U_j = \sum p_i u'(y_i) a_{ij}$, since the ps and the as are all constants. Thus if the $u'(y_i)$ change in equal proportions, the U_j will also change in equal proportions. If they were equal before, they will still be equal.

Now the variable part of this will only be positive, for positive y, if $h < 1$; that is to say the MU curve, in Marshall's sense, must be elastic. If it is inelastic ($h > 1$), the variable part will be negative; so $u(y)$ can only be positive if the constant is large and positive; call this B.

There are thus two cases, according as h is < 1 or $\geqslant 1$. In the former, the variable part of $u(y)$ will be zero when $y = 0$, so we may take that as a base from which to measure; as y increases, through positive values, $u(y)$ will continue to increase. It will increase very rapidly when y is small, thereafter at a diminishing rate. Though this must be given a place in the mathematics,[3] it does not seem to be of much economic interest. It is otherwise with the latter case, where it is proper to write

$$u(y) = B - \frac{A}{h-1} y^{-(h-1)}$$

This I shall claim to be more interesting. Here, as y increases indefinitely, the variable part approaches zero, so that B is a limit beyond which $u(y)$ cannot increase.[4] But if $y = 0$, $u(y)$ is *minus* infinity. This is surprising (in consumer theory it would be nonsense) but I think it makes sense, in the present context.

There is no reason why we should exclude the possibilty of an outcome having a utility of *minus* infinity; for that would just mean that the operator would *always* avoid such an outcome, if it were possible to avoid it. Now if the securities that are on offer are of the usual kinds (bills, bonds and equities carrying limited liability) the worst that can happen from any choice of such securities is total loss of the whole portfolio; that is to say, $y = 0$. To put $u(0)$ equal to minus infinity amounts to saying that a chance of such loss would always be avoided. If there was a particular security for which there was a finite chance of such total loss, to put the whole capital into that security is a course that would always be avoided. To put a part of one's capital into such a security is not a choice that is excluded; for so long as the rest is out into securities where there is no such possibility, there is no chance of total loss over the whole portfolio. It is 'plunging' with

---

[3] In earlier versions of this appendix (as on pp. 251–6 of the second volume of my *Collected Essays*) it was neglected. I have however been persuaded by Stefano Zamagni that I must give it at least this much attention.

[4] So B is the 'bliss' of the famous article by Frank Ramsey on 'Optimum saving' (*Economic Journal*, 1928) which made such an impression on Keynes.

all one's resources which is ruled out. The *minus infinity* of the utility function just means that this obviously foolish behaviour is excluded.

It has thus been shown that there is a quite intelligible utility function which (on Bernoullian principles) is consistent with the distribution of the portfolio, over all securities, remaining unchanged when the capital to be disposed of changes. But, having got so far, we can rather easily get further, indeed much further. We can indeed largely dispense with the help we have got from Bernoulli.

To begin with, why should the disaster point, which is always to be avoided, be set at this purely arithmetical *total loss*? It only looks even apparently plausible to set it at that point, because we have been following the fashion of looking at the money-securities part of the typical balance-sheet in isolation, without regard to other items, real goods on the assets side, and liabilities. If the operator has liabilities as well as assets, or if he is carrying on a productive business which itself creates calls upon him, he may well face disaster, when the outcome of his investments in securities has fallen very low, even if it is not zero. His utility function should then go to *minus infinity* at a positive value of y, which we will call c.

We can deal with this amendment rather easily. We have only to put $u'(y) = A(y - c)^{-h}$, so that the whole MU curve is shifted to the right, becoming asymptotic to $y = c$. The effect of this is very simple. We still have

$$y_i = \sum a_{ij} x_j \qquad \text{and} \qquad K = \sum x_j$$

so that

$$y_i - c = \sum [a_{ij} - (c/K)]x_j$$

Thus maximization is just the same as in the former case, save that all unit outcomes—of particular securities in particular eventualities— are written down by c/K. If K is large compared with c, the write-down is negligible; so the chosen portfolio will be practically the same as with the former function. But as K diminishes, relatively to c, the write-down will take effect. Some of the $a_{ij} - (c/K)$ will then start to go negative, so that the operator will avoid the securities in question, those which have a very low outcome in some eventualities. He will avoid such *risky* securities.

I am at last in a position to go back to Knight. His major distinction, between measureable risks, based on cardinal probabilities (for which there is evidence) and what he calls true uncertainties, which are not so based, I fully accept. Indeed I would now attach much more importance to it than I did in my first contribution to the subject,[5] written under his influence not much more than ten years after his book appeared. That I hope will have been made clear in what precedes.

The chief criticism I would now make of him is that his terminology, which has greatly influenced many subsequent writers, is rather confusing. Our *disaster point* should help to get it straight.

For it suggests that what is needed is a four-way, not a two-way, classification. First, there should be a distinction between choices that involve a *risk* of some sort of disaster—these being just what the plain man would call risky choices—and those which do not. This should be crossed with Knight's distinction between those where the chances are measurable, and those where they are not.

That would give us (1) measurable risky choices, which are those it may be possible to mitigate by some form of insurance; (2) non-measurable risky choices, which probably match the 'true uncertainties' of Knight; (3) measurable non-risky choices, like buying a ticket for a lottery, where the loss involved in not getting a prize is easily bearable; and (4) non-measurable non-risky choices, such as one might think to be involved in the ordinary running of a business. That would seem to make sense. But what it has to do with the 'justification' of profit is another question. I would look for that in a different direction.

If this arrangement is accepted, we do not have to worry whether our actors are 'risk-averse' or not. Every business man must be risk-averse if he is planning to go on with his business. Even the gambler must be risk-averse if he plans to go on with his game. If he has ceased to be risk-averse he has just gone crazy. Risk-aversion is a consequence of rational behaviour, as we have found it to be in the case of banks—and so on.

---

[5] 'Uncertainty and profit' (*Economica*, 1931); reprinted, slightly abridged, in the second volume of my *Collected Essays*.